Jeremiah Newman

RETURN TO THE SACRED

RETURN TO THE SACRED

A SOCIO-RELIGIOUS ANALYSIS

Jeremiah Newman
BISHOP OF LIMERICK

FOUR COURTS PRESS · DUBLIN
LUMEN CHRISTI PRESS · HOUSTON

Printed in Great Britain
for Four Courts Press, Kill Lane,
Blackrock, Co. Dublin
and Lumen Christi Press,
2229 Pech Road, Houston, Texas 77055

ISBN 1-85182-015-9

Contents

Preface 7

Introduction 9

1 Eclipse of the Sacred 19

2 Sociological Aspects of the Church 25

3 The Secularization of Life 41

4 The Privatization of Life 55

5 The Emergence of Civil Religion 91

6 Reintegrating Religion and Life 113

Conclusion 137

Preface

This book is the development of a lecture which I delivered in St Louis, Missouri, in April 1986.

It was presented to an American organization of religious, whose title is the Consortium Perfectae Caritatis. It is not a title that is likely to attract everybody (including some Catholics) in our secularised world, but it is a body that is faithful to the Catholic Church and to the thought of our Pope, John Paul II.

At a time when so many people who call themselves Catholic, yet are not prepared to accord full loyalty to the Church, I hope that this modest contribution to an understanding of today's problems of both society and Church may be helpful.

I wish to thank Father James Viall, the Coordinator of the Consortium, for having invited me to give the lecture (not the first one by me to that body), and the other members of same who made me so welcome and feel at home with them. These are the sort of people that the Catholic Church needs at the present moment of its history and I pray that such will prevail in the true tradition of the Church and succeed in fostering a return to the sacred in life as a whole.

I can only hope that this book will help both religious and laity to recognize the complicated nature of the society in which we live, the pressures, both on ourselves and on the Church of which we are members, and try to come to terms with the clear teaching of Jesus Christ.

+ Jeremiah Newman, Limerick,
8 September 1986,
Feast of the Birthday of the Blessed Virgin Mary.

Introduction

As its sub-title indicates, this book is an essay in socio-religious analysis. Its special interest is the impact on religion — and in particular Christianity — of our present-day society, a society that is imbued with the features of what is known as 'modernity' (something that has always recurred in history but for us today means a new epoch opened up by and for man alone).

The book is, therefore, in the strict sense, an excursion into sociology, not just the sociology that consists of micro-studies, essential though these are for any overall grasp of social reality. Nor is it a study in macro-sociology either, in the sense in which that is commonly understood, namely, a systematic theoretical framework into which micro-studies can be absorbed and reconciled in a broad understanding. While it does take note of both micro data and macro frameworks where necessary or useful, its scope is broader.

For quite some time I have been taken by the need to avoid the study of social matters in a way which the German sociologist Rolf Dahrendorf has described as dealing with man as 'homo sociologicus'[1], that is, man — or rather men and women — who are not real people, with personal reactions and freedom, but rather ciphers and categories — sociological constructs — at the hands of social scientists. One must avoid the error that Adam Smith fell into with his famous 'homo economicus'. As the Austrian sociologist Alfred Shutz put it, for far too long sociological theory has been built up on the basis of models of society that are not inhabited by real people, with individual life experiences, but are simply 'homunculi' created by the sociological scholar to conform to his own systematic vision[2].

This is why the present essay seeks to go beyond systematic sociology, which scarcely treats of the individual as individual or pays any real heed to his everyday experience as consciously experienced by him and to which he reacts. Systematic sociology concentrates on 'social roles', that is, the parts played by individuals in different groups or positions within society, roles that have been constructed by the sociologist on the basis of the interpretation of micro studies of different areas of social behaviour. One cannot complain about that. It has to be like that. Nobody could architect any kind of sociology without attending to the 'nitty gritty' of people's lives, or what the learned would term micro-sociology. The trouble arises when sociology of whatever kind is allowed to take over from common sense and permit theoretical sociologists to 'rule the roost'. They have done so for far too long — despite the efforts of Ralph Linton and C. Wright Mills — with categories and classifications, and well-meaning but unreal interpretations. Ordinary man — integral man — gets lost in that process, for man is many things, plays many roles, as Shakespeare knew well. Man is a person who combines in himself and the society with which he interacts a variety of interrelated factors, both mental and behavioural. He is not, as the role analysis of most systematic sociology would have it, a series of disconnected individuals.

BERGER AND LUCKMANN

If I give any adherence to any school of sociology, it is to a group of European and American scholars by whom I have been influenced considerably. They constitute a school only in the loosest sense, but as their work is not all that old, more may yet come. In any case they have enough followers, so to speak, to warrant linking their approach informally by way of the term 'school'. This approach to the study of man in society puts great emphasis on the wholeness of the individual and of his autonomy in constructing his own world. From that point of view, it has something in common with the personalist philosophy of Emmanuel Mounier and oftentimes resembles a philosophical anthropology. From that point of view too it has a relevance for modern theology.

The point of departure for this way of sociologizing is the world of everyday life and the individual's response to it. It is not a 'world taken for granted', to use a phrase coined by Schutz, of which more below. On the contrary, it is one that is 'cognized' incessantly by people and fashioned by their creativity, yet simultaneously a world that continually pulls them back to reality, to the routines and mundane necessities of daily living[3]. If a title has to be given to this kind of social analysis, one cannot better that of 'Cognitive Sociology'.

It can be said in fairness that, to the extent that this approach to sociology had a 'founder', it was the aforementioned Alfred Schutz (1899-1959). Sometimes spelt Schuetz, this man was an Austrian philosopher of the phenomenological way of thinking, who devoted most of his life's work to the philosophical implications of sociology as a science especially the sociology of knowledge. Having left Austria just before World War II, he taught until his death at the New School for Social Research in New York. Among the most notable of those whom he influenced is Peter Berger, professor of sociology at Boston University. A prolific writer, Berger has produced many books, some in collaboration with his wife, Brigitte Berger, and Hansfried Kellner (of the University of Darmstadt, West Germany), and Thomas Luckmann, professor of sociology at the University of Frankfurt[4]. Luckmann is very influential in his own right. Of Yougoslav origin, he became a U.S. citizen and has taught widely in America, including sociology of religion at the Harvard Divinity School[5]. Although at present professor at Frankfurt, he has no connection with what is called the Frankfurt School of Sociology. In addition to these writers, there are others who have been greatly influenced by Berger and Luckmann. These include notably Anton Zijderveld, professor of sociology at The Tilburg School of Economics in Holland, who has amplified their thought in certain important respects[6].

GOFFMAN

There are still others — not formally connected with those mentioned — whose work links up with theirs in a number of ways, and by whom I have been particularly struck. One of these is Erving Goffman, professor of sociology at the University of Pennsylvania, who, in his own way, has contributed to a unique understanding of the interaction of individuals **inter se** and in their environment, in the conduct of everyday life[7].

Goffman is most usually regarded as a psychiatrist and his work sometimes harshly criticized for concentrating on the micro-structures of interpersonal experiences, to a neglect of the larger and historical framework of social institutions. One finds him charged with pursuing a local and narrowly analytical study of relational behaviour in the settings of small-scale encounters[8]. I believe that this is quite unfair to him, for general sociology is and must be based on more specific studies and, as already noted in the case of Berger and his more immediate associates, it is rooted in the facts of everyday life. Otherwise it is nothing but academic jargon. Goffman himself is aware of this when he says in his book **Frame Analysis**: 'I make no claim whatsoever to be talking about the core matters of sociology — social organization and social structure . . . I am not addressing the structure of social life but the structure of experience individuals have at any moment of their social lives'. One of the things that he has discovered in his perception of the face to face dimensions of human living is the way in which people tend to gravitate towards 'cracks' in the social integument, 'licensed loopholes of idiosyncrasy', as one writer has labelled them, crannies of private integrity.

We shall have occasion to return to all this later. For the moment, let me just say that it links up Goffman's studies with a number of others, rather grandiloquently described in French as **La Psychosociologie de l'Espace**[9]. This is an area of social research which is only lately coming to be appreciated for the important thing it is. In brief it concerns space, not outer space (for the present at least) but the space within which people live and move and conduct their affairs. Of French origin during the 1960's, today it is coming to be accepted as amongst the most advanced and enlightened ways of approaching the problems of social life.

In the Anglo-Saxon world, it has come — at least indirectly — to the attention of many through the writings of Robert Ardrey (**The Territorial Imperative**, London, 1967) about animal reactions to spatial surroundings, of Konrad Lorenz (**On Aggression**, London, 1966), which extends this to human comportment, and of the said Erving Goffman who underlined the fact that spatial configuration and activity has a profound social resonance. Kurt Lewin carried these ideas further. Indeed it is probably fair to say that it is in his work that we find the first scientific bases for a theoretical concept of space as an actual model for social analysis. It was Lewin who, before his time, was responsible for the elaboration of what is now commonly known as 'vital space', that is, the context of interaction between the person and his milieu, embracing all the factors which mould his conduct in any given situation[10].

Yet a further extension of this 'space sociopsychology' has been provided by E.T. Hall in a number of important books, the best known of which is **The Hidden Dimension** [11]. Hall develops the idea of a 'personal space', depicted by some as a kind of portable territory. There is much writing about this nowadays, some of it quite charlatan, regarding 'body buffer zones', 'body language', 'body consciousness', 'body time', and so forth, although by no means is all of it quack stuff. It adds up to the fact that there is such a thing as 'social space' which plays a frighteningly real role in human life.

Anthropologists have begun to accept it and to make use of it in their effort to understand the development of different cultures. Social psychologists too have begun to see 'human space' as one of the principal keys available to the human sciences. Together with the concept of 'time', it is now regarded as a fulcrum of both individual and social activity. In fact, it is coming to be recognized that the notion of space — whether territorial, vital, personal or social — is the most fundamental ground on which inter-individual phenomena run their course. This space is essentially that within which men and women can live and love and die, autonomously: 'Mate, give me space', is the most poignant plea of the contemporary hominoid. In other words, space presents itself as a system of value reference related to man's area of liberty, which may be, and far too often is, enclosed by more or less rigid limits. That is the difficulty in comprehending the anguish of the individual person who feels conditioned by such barriers to self-expression. And it is for precisely this reason that the intuition of people like Goffman and others of the new school of the psychosociology of space is of inestimable value — to the effect that, despite the limits and barriers, there still exists opportunities (whether by ruse or design) for human personalities to escape the straight-jackets of administration, rule, law — call it what you like.

Naturally, not all of these 'escapes' are equally acceptable. It is also true that the imagination plays a large part in the process, for the real use of space is never purely material. But one point does stand out and that is that space, effectively and properly appropriated by him, does give security to the individual (one of the many in Riesman's **The Lonely Crowd**, 1950) and permits him, even in public space, to create certain socially acceptable forms of privatization, the kind of thing that another apt French phrase describes as '**la nidification de l'espace**' — 'nesting', if one prefers that phrase — the construction of a purely personal sphere of activity. Goffman has outlined, better than anybody else that I know of, the ways and means whereby this can be done. That is the reason why I regard him not only as a psychiatrist but also as a sociologist who reflects real life in his writings, and why I add him — and the socio-psychologists of space — to those who have influenced my own thinking quite extensively. We will return to this again, against the background of a discussion of the problem of establishing personal identity (with all that it involves) in our modern world.

The foregoing should suffice to indicate that there is a thread running through these thoughts, that they conform to a pattern, one which derives from some writers who, as I have said, are known to each other and work together, even if not always formally. There are some more too who should be listed as having affected the thought of this book to a greater or lesser degree. These include Rolf Dahrendorf, up to a point, and more importantly Alvin Gouldner, a political sociologist at Washington University, St. Louis, where he is Max Weber Research Professor of Social Theory[12].

GOULDNER

Gouldner is particularly interesting. He is a Marxist of the school of what is called 'Critical Marxism', as against the so called 'Scientific Marxism' of the past. The difference between these is that, whereas the latter relies on the unfolding of ineluctable elements in history, the former appreciates the place of human consciousness — even freedom — in bringing things about, in overcoming the deficiencies of nature and of economic structures. In line with this, Gouldner gives full support to attention to the experience of everyday life under advanced capitalism as a means of understanding and dealing with it[13]. The French Marxist Henri Lefèbvre has written well on this too, quite some years ago[14].

While Christians cannot but have reservations about the Hegelian-Marxist hub of his thought, whether 'pure' or 'revisionist' Marxism, Gouldner's call to consciousness cannot but also find a response in thinkers in as broad a spectrum as one which includes Bergson, Max Scheler and Pope John Paul II, a philosophy which denounces both economic exploitation and sociological dehumanization, with the alienation from and reification of the world which they bring in their train.

Gouldner is not afraid to be a 'sociologist of sociologists'. As such, he completely rejects the 'value free' sociology of my youth (to which by the way I never subscribed). He is at his devastating best when he emphasizes that it is actually necessary for the sociologist to take a standpoint outside that of professional sociology. Far from regarding the sociologist as inevitably 'neutral', he rejects the myth of the value free approach and declares openly that the sociologist not only has a right but a duty to be 'partisan' at least up to a point. He must have a sensitive openness to the 'standpoints' of the 'actors' whom he studies — actors on the world's stage. But that should not deprive him of his own standpoint too. Indeed Gouldner goes so far as to say that 'objectivity is threatened when the actors' standpoints and the sociologists' fuse indistinguishably into one . . . The adoption of an 'outside' standpoint, far from leading us to ignore the participants' standpoint, is probably the only way in which we can even recognize and identify the participants' standpoint'[15].

He does agree that in saying that the explication of the sociologist's value commitment is a necessary condition for his objectivity, we have to recognize the 'grinding difficulties' involved. Not only is it hard oftentimes for the sociologist to know exactly what his own value system is. Even more difficult is the growing transformation of sociology into a 'profession', professions being the kind of bodies that, as such, never, or nearly never, see or want to see personal value commitments (whether to clients, the general public or even human welfare) as critical to their existence and instead treat them as non-problematic 'givens' that they have to reckon with but not at all think of according them professional status. Gouldner just says: 'The development of professionalization among sociologists deserves to be opposed because it undermines the sociologist's capacity for objectivity'[16].

Quite a number of others will be referred to in these pages, who are philosophers or theologians rather than sociologists. To them my gratitude is also due, but I am especially anxious to list those sociologists by whom my thinking has been deeply influenced.

16

All this is by way of acknowledging my indebtedness to these scholars, whether or not they can be classified as members of any particular sociological school or religious affiliation. I too must try to be objective in being 'cognitively aware'.

1 Cf. R. Dahrendorf, **Essays in the Theory of Society** (London, 1968).
2 Cf. A. Schutz, **Collected Papers**, Vol. I (The Hague, 1962), p.41.
3 Cf. Roland Robertson, **The Sociological Interpretation of Religion** (Oxford, 1972).
4 See especially Peter L. Berger, **Invitation to Sociology** (New York, 1963); Peter L. Berger and Thomas Luckmann, **The Social Construction of Reality** (New York, 1966;) **A Rumour of Angels: Modern Society and the Rediscovery of the Supernatural** (New York, 1969); **The Sacred Canopy: Elements of a Sociological Theory of Religion**, (New York, 1969); Peter L. Berger and Brigitte Berger, **Sociology: A Biographical Approach** (New York, 1972); Peter L. Berger, Brigitte Berger and Hansfried Kellner, **The Homeless Mind: Modernization and Consciousness** (New York, 1973); Peter L. Berger, **Pyramids of Sacrifice: Political Ethics and Social Change** (New York, 1974); **Facing up to Modernity: Excursions in Society, Politics, and Religion** (New York, 1977); **The Heretical Imperative: Contemporary Possibilities of Religious Affirmation** (New York, 1979); Peter L. Berger and Hansfried Kellner, **Sociology Reinterpreted** (New York, 1981).
5 See especially, Th. Luckmann, **Das Problem der Religion in der Modernen Gesellschaft** (Freiburg in Breisgau, 1963): English trans. **The Invisible Religion** (New York, 1967); **Phenomenology and Sociology**, (Luckmann ed., New York, 1978), esp. Benita Luckmann, 'The Small Life — Worlds of Modern Man', in the last mentioned book.
6 See Anton Zijderveld, **The Abstract Society: A Cultural Analysis of Our Time** (New York, 1970).
7 See especially Erving Goffman, **The Presentation of Self in Everyday Life** (New York, 1959); **Interaction Ritual: Essays on Face to Face Behaviour** (New York, 1967); **Frame Analysis: An Essay on the Organization of Experience** (New York, 1974).
8 Cf. Peter Sedgwick, **Psycho Politics** (New York, 1982).
9 Cf. Gustave-Nicolas Fischer, **La Psychosociologie de l'Espace** (Paris, 1981).
10 Cf. K. Lewin, **Principles of Topological Psychology** (New York, 1936).
11 New York, 1969. See also by the same author: **The Silent Language** (New York, 1959).
12 Cf. Alvin Gouldner, **For Sociology: Renewal and Critique in Sociology Today** (London, 1973). Also **The Future of Intellectuals and the Rise of the New Class** — the second volume of a trilogy: 'Marxist — non Marxist' (New York, 1979).

13 Cf. **For Sociology**, pp. 440-441.
14 Cf. Henri Lefèbvre, **La vie quotidienne dans le monde moderne** (Paris, 1968).
15 **For Sociology**, pp. 56-57.
16 Ibid., p. 61.

1

Eclipse of the Sacred

Early in 1986 a book was published in Paris, with the title **L'Éclipse du Sacré**[1]. It is the product of a discussion between two philosophers, Thomas Molnar, a 'European' Catholic and Alain de Benoist, a 'Graeco-Roman' Heideggerian. I know that these designations do not do full justice to either man, but, as will shortly emerge, they are meaningful.

Both Molnar and Benoist are in agreement that the 'sacred' is something that has been largely lost in modern times. Simultaneously, both of them differ deeply in their understanding of what the sacred means and why it has been largely lost. Despite that, indeed possibly because of it, their exchange of views is one of the most brilliant and compelling pieces of literature that has appeared for quite some time.

THOMAS MOLNAR

It is not my function or purpose here to try to summarise their book, but it does seem to me to be necessary to present its basic concepts before engaging myself in an investigation of the sacred in contemporary life.

Molnar's attitude is that the desacralization of life is currently effected first of all through ideologies, which ignore the transcendental dimension of existence and concentrate on technology and all that it represents by way of 'enlightened self-interest', the 'electoral system' and the decisions of experts' — all of which are regarded as the **ne plus ultra** of advanced Western society, a society in and through which man engages in an auto-sacralization that excludes God. Secondly, Molnar says, desacralization is effected through the cult of 'things', the products of industrialization, 'objects' being a better term for them, which have come to dominate almost everything, from former 'sacred' places and even times to the still struggling sacred places and times of today (the Ganges, Christmas, the great cathedrals . . .). He mounts a powerful argument based on the lack of any unicity in present-day production, a lack which yields but 'gadgets', of which the whole world is over full, especially those '**societés de consommation**' of our day. Thirdly, Molnar points out that the process of desacralization is also pushed along by the multiplication of images today — images in the wide sense of that term. It is a process which contributes to the banalization of just about everything.

Believer though he is, Molnar can be quite critical of some aspects of Christianity. Of one thing he is strangely convinced, and that is that Christianity itself has played a part (as practised by its adherents) in desacralization by furthering the sacralizing of history, that is, of man himself. What he has in mind is people like Darwin, Hegel, Marx and many others who, whatever their origin or proclaimed religion, were undoubtedly influenced by Christianity in a way that has made for a 'modernity' that is not at all helpful to the religion that gave it birth. The Catholic Church as such has been affected by this — especially through the separation of Church and State, first in France and later elsewhere, and today culminating in the attempt by some to separate Church and Society. To the extent that this kind of thing succeeds, the Church becomes 'marginal' to society. It is sad that Jacques Maritain, one of whose early and marvellous books was **The Primacy of the Spiritual**[2], should, after a sojourn in the U.S.A., come to agree with the interdenominational society to be found there to an extent which, if followed out fully, would make the Church rather irrelevant to temporal society.

Molnar goes beyond this, saying that Christianity is to some extent a cause of desacralization through the rationalism and mechanism which have come to overshadow modern life. He has in mind especially those progressive theologians of liberation, of process, of politics, etc., who know no God but an abstract entity, certainly not the God of Jesus Christ. The 'fruit' of that approach could not be other than a search for a new 'sacred', whether through astrology, electronic phantasmagoria, or — and this is on our doorsteps — the sacralization of the State and of political parties, even in the 'democratic' State. There is no question but that Molnar is drawing a long bow in his criticism and that he means to do so, in order to draw out Benoist. Let us see what the latter has to say.

ALAIN DE BENOIST

Benoist is the exact opposite, intellectually, to Molnar, even though the two of them can agree on certain basic matters. For Benoist the sacred is conceptually linked with Levy-Bruhl's idea that it is essentially a 'relational' thing, an association between a heaven of the 'gods' and an earth that is the haven of people and others, both visible and invisible. He is inseparable from the religions of antiquity — of Greece and Rome — which were identified not so much with belief but with cult, a cult which confirmed one also as citizen (as Fustel de Coulanges made so clear many years ago in his magisterial work **La Cité Antique**[3]). It was a cult that embraced both time and place, a cult that mediated the sacred in and through nature — the divine repository of praeternatural powers of one kind or another.

Benoist also says (although not at all in the way Molnar teases) that the sacred has been destroyed by the Judaeo-Christian religion, which, as his thesis runs, created a cosmos distinct from God (he would have been truer to his own thinking if he had said 'gods'). For Benoist (who acknowledges his ancestral Christian origins), Christianity denounces all forms of 'natural religiosity' as idolatry. In company with some Existentialists of more recent times, he would have us believe that the Christian is primarily a citizen of another world (something related to St Augustine's **City of God**). It is not unlike what Maurice Merleau-Ponty wrote about St Paul's interpretation of Christianity[4]. In common with Molnar's 'pinching' suggestions, Benoist would argue that the 'ancient city' of F. de Coulanges was directly linked with images that projected the sacred (not literally but symbolically). They presented man, not only as a 'political animal' and 'rational animal' but also as a 'sentimental animal', that is, a being that is capable of non rational (I do not say irrational) thought and feelings — a **presence sensible**, as only the French language can put it, to the image, the **eidolon**, as the Greeks would put it, in statues, sanctuaries, temples, which incarnated the sacred. In that sense, the sacred unavoidably involves 'idolatry'.

For Benoist, a desacralized world is an 'inanimate' world, a world 'makeable' by man to his own image and likeness, a world in which man's objects by their very nature are 'inanimate'. Benoist sees the world as 'alive', alive with the forces and deities of the classical period on which he is an expert and which he upholds.

Talking about **La Cité Antique**, there is a point that Benoist also discerns. It concerns the devaluation of politics. True, his way to discovering this is not the way that everybody would follow. He rather overdoes the revolt of the Hebrews against the Egyptians, their breakaway and emancipation from (one) politico-sacral power — to such an extent that his propositions about Judaeo-Christianity devaluing the political scene may seem exaggerated.

To that he adds the contention that Christianity has favoured the disappearance of sacred times and places that used to be. All is connected with the central message that monotheism (as against the gods and godesses of the ancient past) has led to the elimination of the sacred by way of seeing the world and nature only as a conglomeration of material objects. As Benoist says, 'Yaweh is not the god of any place'. For Benoist monotheism, and specifically its Christian expression, has led inevitably, first to Cartesian subjectivity, later to the minimal sacramentality of the Reformation, then to the Wars of Religion (involving the setting up of the State's new foundation quite outside of faith). This was the beginning of Secularization, to be followed by the Enlightenment, when Christianity came down to earth to be sure but with no spirituality. It ended, for the time being at any rate, with Kant and Hegel, who divorced reason from faith.

Benoist is well aware of the consequences of that evolution. He says, and rightly, that the 'sacred' is something that cannot be explained, that it has in it something of the 'irrational', even though at the same time he subscribes to the notion that to treat any object (that is, any part of nature) simply as an object is to 'desacralize' it. He is quite acute in his delineation of our secularized society, in which he sees the extent to which faith no longer organizes that society, in which 'things' are no longer significant for their own intrinsic worth, no longer 'mystical', in the right sense of that word, and in which religion has become an entirely private affair for very many people.

I hope the reader will notice that I have not attempted at this stage to criticize either Molnar or Benoist. They are clearly fine scholars. Yet they are poles apart in their thinking. At the end of the book, I will try to offer some comments relating to what both of them are saying. At the moment, it is evident to me that, if I am going to try to deal with the question of the sacred in sociological language (but necessarily, as far as I am concerned, within the framework of Catholic Christianity), I must begin to write about the Church as 'mystery'. Because no matter what the pundits may say, that is the primary nature of the Church of Our Lord Jesus Christ.

1 Editions La Table Ronde.
2 Paris, 1927. English transl. **The Things that are not Caesar's** (London, 1930). See Maritain's **Reflections on America** (New York, 1958) and **Man and the State** (English ed. 1954).
3 First published in 1864, it still remains one of the finest — if not the finest — treatises of its kind. Published in English in 1873.
4 In **Sens et Non-Sens** (Paris, 1948).

2

Sociological Aspects of the Church

A discussion on the use of sociology for endeavouring to attain some insights into the mystery of the Christian Church calls for a preliminary word on the Church as mystery.

THE CHURCH AS MYSTERY

The term 'mystery' itself derives from a Hebrew word which signifies something hidden, something beyond the understanding of men. In the Septuagint its Greek equivalent occurs some twenty or so times. It occurs in the New Testament, especially the Epistles of St Paul. In the Gospels it is used in both the singular and the plural, in relation to the mysteries of God in general and the mystery of the Kingdom of God in particular. St Paul gives it more elaborate application. Taking the New Testament as a whole, it can be said that the term 'mystery' is employed basically to connote the inscrutable plan of God for the salvation of man.

Small wonder then that we should find the concept of mystery employed from patristic times onward in theological expositions of the Christian religion, and in an extensive way in seeking to outline the nature of the Church. In modern times this approach was spectacularly underlined in 1865 with the publication of the German theologian Scheeben's great work entitled **The Mysteries of Christianity**[1], of which a new edition in English was brought out in St Louis in 1951. Scheeben's lead was followed by another famous work, **The Mystery of Faith**[2], a study of the Mass by the French Jesuit

Maurice de la Taille, and later by a study of the Church, **The Mystery of the Church**[3], from the contemporary Dominican theologian Yves Congar. Indeed after the publication of the Encyclical on the Church as the Mystical Body of Christ [4] by Pope Pius XII in 1943, there was quite a spate of writing on the Church viewed from the angle of mystery. It was only natural and logical, therefore, that Vatican II's **Dogmatic Constitution on the Church**[5] should have as its opening chapter a statement on 'The Mystery of the Church'.

THE CHURCH AS HUMAN

And yet, despite this emphasis on the part of theology and the magisterium on the mysterious, mystical, sacred, supernatural, transcendent — and therefore in a certain sense superhuman and indefectible — nature of the Church, we all know the extent to which that same Church for the past quarter of a century has been buffeted by internal discord and worldly forces. Book after book has appeared with titles such as **The Human Church, The Underground Church, The Contested Church, The Church in a State of Mortal Sin, The Broken Church, The Runaway Church, The Vulnerable Church**, and so on[6].

These go to show that, notwithstanding its supernatural and mysterious side, the Church is also very much rooted in this world and affected by what happens in the world. That, of course, was always known. It has always been theological orthodoxy that grace does not destroy nature and that, as a result, individual men and society as a whole are capable of weakness and sin. At the same time, I think it true to say that until recently the emphasis has been on the supernatural aspects of the Church, to a relative neglect of its human side, an emphasis on the Church as a divine institution to a soft-pedalling of it as a human society. I think it true to say also that the Second Vatican Council, in the second chapter of its **Dogmatic Constitution on the Church**, headed 'The People of God', sought somewhat to adumbrate the historical aspect of the Church, as a community rooted in the vicissitudes of time. It is latter-day sociology, however, that has most enthusiastically taken up the exploration of the Church from this human and societal viewpoint.

MODELS OF THE CHURCH

I would like to examine a little how this is attempted. Theology itself has pointed the way through the study of the Church by using models. This was advanced in the 1974 publication, **Models of the Church**, by Fr Avery Dulles[7]. While acknowledging that the Church is indeed a mystery, meaning that it is not in its entirety fully intelligible to man's finite mind, Fr Dulles recognizes, in accordance with Pope Paul VI's opening address to the second session of Vatican II, that it lies 'within the very nature of the Church to be always open to new and ever greater exploration'. In that connection, Dulles points out, very fruitfully, that, even though the mysterious nature of the Church rules out the possibility of encompassing it in clear and univocal concepts, at the same time this should not cause us to adopt a negative stance towards the Church, 'affirming not what it is but only what it is not'. For even though such an approach does have to be followed up to a point, we must not neglect the possibilities of a positive stance towards its comprehension.

Among the positive tools that have been used to this end, are, he says, what may be called 'models'. Models are another word for developed images. They constitute intellectual frames or frameworks within which some grasp of their subject may be had, just as does, to take a simple example, the use of the term 'flock' to convey the relationship of his people to Christ. Such images, when employed reflectively and critically, can deepen one's understanding of what they signify. They can become what the English theologian I.T. Ramsey, former Bishop of Durham, whom I knew personally many years ago when I was a student in Oxford, also called models, in his remarkable work **Models and Mystery**[8]. They provide conceptual and linguistic instruments that embrace and hold together in a whole what would otherwise be opaque to anything beyond piecemeal intellection.

THEOLOGICAL MODELS

Dulles himself proposes five models for use by theological ecclesiologists. These are: the Church as institution, the Church as community, the Church as sacrament, the Church as herald of the Gospel, and the Church as the servant of man. Each of these classifications has had and still has its exponents, because each of them represents a valid glimpse of the Church. In recent times, I suppose there has been no more able exponent of the Church as a hierarchical system than Charles Journet, in his learned work **The Church of the Word Incarnate**, first published in 1935[9]. As a community, and a mystical community at that, the Church has found able projection in the already mentioned work of Fr Yves Congar, as well as that of Fr Jerome Hamer, now Jerome Cardinal Hamer of the Sacred Congregation for Religious[10]. The Church as sacrament has found lucid articulation in Scheeben's work as well as in the more recent study of Otto Semmelroth, **The Church as Primordial Sacrament**[11]). As herald of the Gospel, the Church has found theological conceptualisation to some extent in the work of the Lutheran theologian, Karl Barth, whose emphasis on the Word was taken up by Hans Küng, in his book **The Church**[12]. Fifthly and lastly, there are the many proponents — notably in current times — of the Church as servant. We will come back to them later. They are chiefly those who are concerned with what Dulles speaks about the Church in its secular or dialogic dimension, concerned with adapting to the world and seeking an end to a sacred-profane distinction. On the Protestant side Bonhoeffer and the Catholic side Teilhard de Chardin come to mind immediately as examples of this reformist way of thinking[13]. Harvey Cox, John Robinson, Thomas Altizer and Paul van Buren have carried it to its extremity[14]. Their sentiments have at times been echoed by lesser writers, such as Bishops Jenkins and Habgood, and Don Cupitt.

There is some divergence of view as to which of these theological models towards an understanding of the Church is the most appropriate, but the general consensus is that each of them has its own insight to impart. Indeed, it is generally recognized that all of them have their place in any effort to seek to elucidate the theological essence of the Church.

What I would like to explore briefly here is whether the human side of the Church is capable of being subjected to scrutiny in some analogous way, I mean by way of the human sciences and, in the concrete, sociology, the science of society.

A SOCIOLOGICAL MODEL?

The noted European sociologist, Alfred Schutz, has maintained that all sociological theory is built up out of analytic models relating to people in social situations as viewed by the sociologist[15]. Given that way of thinking, sociological theory concerning the Church would have no option but to resort to models of one kind or another, along lines kindred to those followed by theology even though of a different intellectual pattern. Whether this be the case or not, a more basic question is whether any sociological probing can in any way illuminate our ideas about the Church — that mystery of God's salvation of men, which also exists in an existential human and historical situation.

This question arises precisely because of the specificity of the Church, that is, its uniqueness as a social entity, at one and the same time divine and human, sacred and profane, supernatural and natural, transcendental and secular. This does indeed create a difficulty for sociology as applied to the Church of Christ. For, though the sacred — as we know from anthropology — is in itself something separable from the positively religious sphere, as in the case of magic, voodoo, taboo and the like, and can sometimes even become associated with aesthetics and politics, in which contexts it does not at all consist of the mediation of the divine to men, whenever it signifies any true religious reference it involves a special dimension[16]. That dimension is something nearly all writers about the sacred admit that they cannot fathom. Many terms are used to try to describe it — the fascinating, the tremendous, the dreadful, the awful, but never the commonplace. There is general agreement, though, that the sacred (**sacer**) and holy (**sanctus**) are related, the latter stemming from a mysterious human intervention, the first resulting from that, but equally mysterious in itself. And for the Christian as against the pagan, both of these have their ultimate source in the intervention of the divine. All genuine religion has such specificity, being centered on God and not just on what Rudolph Otto called 'the numinous' [17], which has a wider connotation. It demands a subjective faith on the part of its adherents that is not always required in other domains of the sacred which are satisfied with the performance of external rites.

Given these animadversions, the question becomes pressing as to whether and how sociological methodology can touch religion. The point has been made frequently that, of necessity, by reason of its own intellectual assumptions, sociological theory has got to look upon religion as a purely human phenomenon, with no reference to anything other than its human origins. In other words, the methodology of sociology is, by its very nature, a 'methodological atheism'. Still, in that capacity, it is not necessarily an anti-religious discipline. Like science in general, it can claim to be, and often is, truly neutral in its stance (although all too often it can also betray both unconscious assumptions and value judgements that render its neutral posturing null and void). The best practitioners of the subject assure us that sociology should not unduly worry the theologian, **qua** theologian, because it can be employed objectively. At the same time, even those who defend this attitude are ready to agree that it would be foolish to maintain that theological positions are entirely immune to injury from sociology[18]. Sociology can raise issues concerning the socio-historical wrappings of theology in a way that can inevitably affect it.

LIMITS OF MODELS

While this is true, we must also keep other considerations in mind. One is that theological investigations are dependent on revelation and are not in themselves empirically verifiable. Nor is the fact that theologians are historically conditioned in their approach to the investigation of their subject matter any more relevant than is the case with other disciplines. At any rate, even though some sociologists might like to think so, theological propositions are not in their essence grounded on human infrastructures, no more than religious experience derives its credibility from the exigencies of the social fabric at any given time. Theological utterances, in their dogmatic content, are not purely human formulations, notwithstanding the efforts of some modern Liberal Protestant theology to give the impression that they are historically conditioned to the point of being basically relative.

There still remains an area — I will not call it a no man's land of investigation — a grey area, so to speak, in which sociological searching can throw some light on the human and societal aspects of religion in general and, in particular, the Church. Nobody has put this better than the American sociologist Peter Berger when he says: 'An "empirical theology" is, of course, methodologically impossible. But a theology that proceeds in a step-by-step correlation with what can be said about man empirically is well worth a serious try'[19]. This means that even though theology is not subject to empirical disconfirmation, it can provide material for valid and useful empirical observations. This is especially the case about the Church as a human society. One does not have to endorse any named ideology in order to realise that religious developments at the human level, such as what are called crises for religion and the Church, may appear to be purely spiritual or intellectual in origin, but in fact always have a social background. Indeed one could go further and say that, very often, they are part and parcel of social crises, by which I mean profound changes in society — sometimes the result of force (political or otherwise) but not always so. Human society is subject to change for diverse reasons of which, of course, individual responsibility is part.

This brings us back to the question as to whether a sociological model for ecclesiological employment can be elaborated? Let us take three models that have been advanced respectively by Marxism, Structuralism and the Sociology of Knowledge.

THE MARXIST MODEL

That of Marxism is mentioned only for the purpose of elimination from meaningful socio-religious discourse. This is because, in all classical and post-classical integral Marxist thought, religion is treated as an alienation of man from God, or as some call it a reification, that is, an objectifying of a human wish for security — 'the sigh of the oppressed creature', as Marx himself put it. The Marxist model for the exploration of religion, in any of its elaborations, treats **religion as an illusion**. To quote from Marx again: 'The abolition of religion, as the illusory happiness of men, is a demand for their real happiness. The call to abandon their illusions about their condition is a call to abandon a condition which requires illusions'[20]. For Marxist sociology of religion — whether crude or sophisticated — that is the inescapable starting-point.

The Marxist system is inextricably founded on a dialectic of contradictions, between opposed elements, in every segment of social analysis. That is its Hegelian heritage. It can be applied to the Church in various ways. One of the most popular with Marxists is the dichotomy between the Church as a clerical preserve, as it were, and the Church as a lay involvement. In this perspective, much has been made from time to time by Marxists of a sociological model which turns on a polarisation between an intellectual, liturgical, sacramental, administrative, educational, etc. zone of clerical activity, and a passive zone of lay receptivity. The point is made that the Church is culturally trapped in an antithetic dualism by reason of its consolidation in feudal times along the lines of a bifocal class distinction. Following this line, it is said, to take just two instances, that the recent decline in religious vocations is not really due to a lack of generosity and the like on the part of youth, but to the fact that nowadays the priesthood and religious life in its totality no longer constitutes a social value in a consciously laicised Church, and also that in liturgical celebration, although now given a new disposition by way of the use of the vernacular and the corporeal postures of the ecclesiastical ministers, the faithful no longer 'follow' in that they do not see any real correspondence between the functions of the ministry and their own personal religious attitudes.

In Marxist sociology this is assembled in the thesis that the Church is imprisoned in a historical model which applies to the Western world as a whole; it is caught between its ancestry and its modern situation. A fundamental tension is claimed to exist within it between its hierarchical institutional reality and that of its lay, democratic, community reality. On the part of Christians affected by this outlook, it is only to be expected that there should be a reaction aimed at breaking those inherited Church-State relations which are seen to support the opposed clerical-lay position. And so we witness in some quarters the emergence of a Liberation Theology that has for its practical counterpart, revolution, in the name of Church emancipation from the past.

Any such Marxist-type analysis of social history calls for a rereading of the Gospels in terms of the fostering of a rupture with the established order, absolute condemnation of its upholders and a corresponding support for its antagonists. Whatever one calls these opposites — whether the ensconced and the dispossessed, the powerful and the flotsam of events, the rich and the poor, the 'haves' and the 'have-nots' — does not matter very much. What does matter, and matter vitally, is that Marxist sociological analysis in its very essence, while being antithetical to religious interests, is also responsible for the generating of a revolutionary Christian initiative wherever it has influenced Christianity. One has only to peruse the writings of the Frankfurt School of sociology — those of Max

Horkeimer, Theodor Adorno, Herbert Marcuse and others [21] — to realise how they have influenced the theological writings of Jurgen Moltmann, Gustavo Gutierrez, Jon Sobrino and suchlike[22]. Moltmann has worked out what he calls a 'political theology of the cross'; Gutierrez a rather more than purely theological vision of the 'escathological power of the poor' in human history, and Sobrino a somewhat tendentious concept of 'solidarity' for Christians. Juan Luis Segundo is something else.

THE STRUCTURALIST MODEL

A second sociological model of the Church that has been elaborated over the last couple of decades is what might be called a structuralist one. Not that Structuralism is, in any way, along the lines say of idealism or pragmatism or existentialism, a philosophical or ideological system, with a holistic content of its own. Rather is it the case that Structuralism is first and last a methodology that is capable of application in diverse fields of study. As one writer about it has said, 'structuralism is not a creed but a method'[23]. It is a particular way of approaching a subject-matter, whether in anthropology, history, literary criticism, sociology. Its characteristic method of rationalising the data of any of these disciplines is to employ a certain linguistic analysis (they call it semiology in Europe and semiotics in the United States) to the elucidation of what it deals with. The primordial tool of the structuralist is that of 'language', that is, of 'sign' or 'signification', and as employed by the sociology of religion, it places much emphasis on the fact that many of the words used in talking abut God may be disappearing from the vocabulary of large sections of society.

This approach is objective in that it takes up the 'given real', that is, **religion as behaviour**, and tries to explain its significance. One of the chief intimations of the structuralist analysis of religion is to communicate the view that the Church as a social model cannot function except in congruence with its social surroundings, and that the crises that envelop it today must be seen as a reflection of all those social changes which affect the world as a whole, and more immediately the Western world, in which Christianity had its cradle. In the case of the Church, this type of analysis is used by structuralists in a way which, even though it is not at all the Marxist one, equally recognises a model reflective of the dominance of the hierarchical and clerical institution vis-a-vis the lay community. And there is no doubt but that one can take up such a model meaningfully. Between Trent and Vatican II, the visceral social relations within the Church have certainly been structured in such a way as to underline the existence of this bilateral situation. Without regarding it as a contradictory polarisation in the way that Marxist sociology does, it is possible to see in the Church, as it developed over the past few centuries, a growing animosity (for lack of a better term) between the 'priest-actor' and the 'lay-spectator' in many ecclesiological sectors.

In that scenario, what appears to be the most significant development has been the gradual but persistent cleavage between religion and civil life, beginning with the separation of Church and State, but continuing with the accrescence of a new cultural humanism, a prolongation of the earlier Renaissance humanism, which placed great weight on the convictions of the individual. This latter, it is said, led to a one-track effort in the Church since the Counter-Reformation to return things to what they were before, but an effort which was overtaken by events. Thus, the argument goes, the Catholic world sustained a social trauma, which has contributed greatly to its present impasse[24].

Many examples are advanced to sustain this claim. It is pointed out that the consent in Catholic marriage, with all its traditional implications, has become for many only a verbal formula, the question of its indissolubility now widely hinging on the meaning that is attached to the exchange of consent. More basically, we are told, the saying of the 'Our Father' has become irrevelant for those who, in common with their generation, have come to query the notion and implications of paternity and who have many nutritional options other than seeking just daily bread. The notion of 'church' too does not always correspond in present-day Christendom to that of a sacred place — church buildings being often regarded as places not only or even primarily for cult but for all sorts of secular community functions. For some people, even the very idea of Christ ascending into heaven is said to have become somewhat obfuscated by the achievements of the astronauts.

Devout practitioners of the faith may say that this kind of speculation is going too far. What they may not fully realise is that what has been referred to or something like it has in actual fact for some time been gnawing at the heart of Catholic practice. Statues have long been discarded in many churches; in some places, the crib has found a substitute in poor-boxes honed in to the needs of the Third World; the tabernacle, the ciborium and the monstrance have sometimes disappeared; chalices have all too often become commonplace pottery artefacts. Candles are at times dispensed with, as is also incensation, where once the norm, and genuflection before the Blessed Sacrament. Communion on the tongue is abhorrent to many, and people often sit for most of the Mass. The most recent (July, 1986) example of a frenetic attempt at **aggiornamento** has been the commissioning by the French Catholic National Committee for Sacred Art of the **haute couture** designers André Courrèges and Jean-Charles Castelbajac to create new-style vestments for the clergy of the future. Whether the designers were believers or not did not matter. That is all right. It has often happened before in history, even as recently as the pontificate of Pope John XXIII. But the 'boiler-suit' design for an alb, produced by Courrèges, and Castelbajac's choice of colours for a chasuble left many of the faithful gasping, despite the well-intentioned efforts of the promoters to make the 'signs' of Christianity more 'meaningful'.

These things in themselves do not constitute a massive problem. I am not one of those fundamentalist, squarish people, who go in for an obscurantist regressivism. I do believe in reasonable liberalism, a conservative liberalism, if you like. The real problem is when there is thought to be no problem, simply because there is no awareness, precisely because the mystery which those matters to which I have referred symbolised has evaporated — been vaporised as they say in current science fiction. All these developments within the Church — and who can deny that they have occurred? — do leave the Church as behaviour, examined from a structuralist position, open to much criticism, even to scepticism about its supernatural claims. For all that, Christians should not forget that, just like Marxist sociological analysis, that of Structuralism is also handicapped, even mortally wounded, in its attempt at a comprehensive human analysis of the Church. One shrewd English commentator has written of it: 'The Christian sociologist, while he dares not ignore the problems thrown up by this kind of sociological study, will approach them with his own presuppositions . . . . On language, the answer, for the Christian, can never . . . abandon any hint of "redemption", "sacrifice" or "atonement"'[25].

THE COGNITIVE MODEL

We come now to a third — and, for our present purpose, final — model for a sociological investigation of the Church. I am speaking of what might be called a 'cognitive model'. This is an approach by way of looking at **religion as belief**, a subjective approach in itself, yet at the same time one that is rooted in the objective reality of societal developments. I am referring especially to the work of Peter Berger and his associates, who make the case — and a good one it is — that the positivist proclivity towards facticity in sociology has led to a neglect of the subjective realm of social reality, in other words, an ignoring of religion as belief. Berger and Co. place the sociology of religion (including that of the Church) in the context of the sociology of knowledge[26].

If one were to sum up this approach, one would say that religion is a social construct, to the extent that its formulas and rituals are geared to a projection by its adherents of a reality that corresponds with their social experience. Therefore, religion can in a certain sense and up to a certain point be sociologically 'explained'. It should not really have to be pointed out that such an approach, taken in and confined to itself, cannot do justice to religion as belief. The same English commentator that I have quoted already says (he is David Lyon of the Social Science School of the University of Bradford in England): 'The sociological study of religion-as-belief needs much clarification: the Christian is bound to tackle it in a different way from the unbeliever'[27].

Nonetheless, it seems to me that Berger's way of looking at things is not without considerable validity. From him and his colleague, Thomas Luckmann, and others, there has emerged a conceptual model which, at one and the same time, can go far towards comprehending the objective or behavioural and the subjective or notional aspects of the human side of religion and the Church. Luckmann puts it well when he scouts the idea of 'ultimate relevance', meaning the fabric of social consciousness whereby individual religious consciousness is basically sustained. As he puts it, 'the subjective system of "ultimate" relevance — always retaining its reference to the objective sacred cosmos — serves to legitimate and justify explicitly the subjective pattern of priorities' of the individual[28].

As a limited exposition, this contains a lot of truth. Indeed I think that both the structuralist and the cognitive sociological models can be useful in promoting some understanding of the human side of the Church. True, they are experimental and as such open to question. Also none of them touches, nor can touch, the inner core of the Church. When one thinks it over, however, one comes to realise that limits (if not the same, at least analogous) are also imposed on non-empirical human scratchings at the indiscipherable reality of religion and the Church — I mean philosophy and theology.

1   M. J. Scheeben, **Die Mysterien des Christentums** (Freiburg,1865).
2   M. de la Taille, SJ, **Esquisse du Mystère de la Foi** (Paris, 1937).
3   Yves Congar, OP, **Esquisses du Mystère de l'Église**, (Paris, 1937).
4   Pope Pius XII, Enc. **Mystici Corporis Christi**, 1943.
5   Vatican II, Dogm. Const. **Lumen Gentium**.
6   Cf. William H. DuBay, **The Human Church** (New York, 1964); Malcolm Boyd (ed.), **The Underground Church**, (New York, 1968); Jacques Marny, **L'Église Contestée** (Paris, 1968); Henri Fesquet, **Une Église en état de peché mortel** (Paris, 1968); R. Dulong, **Une Église Cassée**, (Paris, 1971); Peter Hebblethwaite, **The Runaway Church** (London, 1975); Gerard Defois, **Vulnerable et Passionnante Église** (Paris, 1977).
7   Avery Dulles, SJ, **Models of the Church** (New York, 1974; 1978). See also J.F. O'Grady, **Models of Jesus** (New York, 1981).
8   New York, 1964.
9   Ch. Journet, **L'Église du Verbe Incarné** (Paris, 1935).
10 Congar, op.cit.; J. Hamer, **The Church is a Communion** (New York, 1965).
11 O. Semmelroth, **Die Kirche als Ursakrament** (Frankfurt, 1953).
12 H. Küng **Die Kirche**, (Freiburg im Breisgau, 1967). English translation **The Church**, (London, 1967).
13 Cf. D. Bonhoeffer, **Letters and Papers**, English version (Munich, 1951); P. Teilhard de Chardin, **Le Phénomène Humain** (Paris, 1955).
14 H. Cox, **The Secular City** (New York, 1965); J.A.T. Robinson, **The New Reformation?** (Philadelphia, 1965); Th. Altizer, **Toward a New Christianity** (New York,1968); P. van Buren, **The Secular Meaning of the Gospel** (New York, 1963). See also L. Morris, **The Abolition of Religion** (London, 1964).
15 Cf. A. Schutz, **Collected Papers**, Vol. I. (The Hague, 1962).
16 Cf. Jean-Jacques Wunenburger, **Le Sacré** (Paris, 1981).
17 Cf. R. Otto, **Das Heilige** (published in Germany in 1917; first English edition, **The Idea of the Holy**, 1923).
18 Cf. Peter Berger, **The Sacred Canopy: Elements of a Sociological Theory of Religion** (New York, 1967).
19 Berger, op. cit., p. 185.
20 Cf. T. B. Bottomore and M. Rubel, **Karl Marx: Selected Readings in Sociology and Social Philosophy** (London, 1976).
21 For suitable extracts from the works of these sociologists see Paul Connerton, ed., **Critical Sociology** (London, 1967).
22 Cf. Jurgen Moltmann, **Der gekreuzigte Gott** (Munich, 1973); Gustavo Gutierrez, **Teología de la liberación** (Lima, 1971); Jon Sobrino, **Teología de la solidaridad cristiana** (Managua, 1983).
23 John Sturrock, ed., **Structuralism and Since: from Levi-Strauss to Derrida** (Oxford, 1979), p.2.
24 Cf. R. Dulong, **Une Église Cassée** (Paris, 1971); P. Debray, **Les Technocrates de la Foi** (Paris, 1968); J. Hitchcock, **Catholicism and Modernity** (New York, 1979).
25 David Lyon, **Christians and Sociology** (London 1975), pp. 75-76.

26 See especially Berger and Luckmann, **The Social Construction of Reality**, (New York, 1966).
27 Lyon, op.cit., 80.
28 Th. Luckmann, **Das Problem der Religion in der Modernen Gesellschaft** (Freiburg, 1963); English translation: **The Invisible Religion** (New York, 1967), 71.

3

The Secularization of Life

Assuming that, allowing for their limitations, the social sciences, prudently used, can provide some useful peeps into the Church as a human entity, let us probe a little into what they have to offer. The possibilities open in this respect are numerous. There is one development that has made the most forceful social impact on the Church in our time and which, more than any other, calls for attention. I am speaking about 'secularization'. Many definitions of secularization have been advanced, some too intricate to be of any use. For me it means simply and solely the abandonment of any real belief in God, firstly in so far as belief can be given application in public life and, eventually, in that of the individual. For one cannot really separate one's public and private 'persona'. In all its forms, secularization is a prime feature of today's world and Church and has got to be faced up to.

TECHNOLOGISM

Facing up to it requires an effort to ascertain its roots. These are many, because the secular is itself multi-faceted. I don't think we will be wrong however if we say that secularization began as an offshoot of our modern world. I mean by that, in the first place, the kind of corporative industrial and business enterprise that was originally delineated by Peter Drucker[1], afterwards as so-called post-industrial society by Daniel Bell[2], and as technological society by Jacques Ellul[3].

When one pieces these together, one realises that they

represent the culmination of what was pioneered in the pre-World War II period and during the war by Burnham in his pace-setting work **The Managerial Revolution**, and by Hayek in **The Road to Serfdom**[4]. It was given more practical advancement in Hitler's Germany by the economic National Socialism of Dr Schacht, Finance Minister to the Third Reich, in America by the architects of President Roosevelt's New Deal, and in Britain by J.M. Keynes, who was the economic prefigurator of the Welfare State[5]. All of these brought the State more and more into dominating the life of the individual. They were responsible for the 'socialisation' of life in the sense recognised by Pope John XXIII's encyclical **Mater et Magistra**[6]. In other words, the political machine and/or the corporation took over. In the Soviet Union the same thing occurred, only in a more drastic fashion. From the point of view of society as a whole, there is not that much difference between the evolution that has taken place in all quarters of the developed world.

It would appear that it was Anthony Jay who first spoke about 'corporate tribes' in his book **Corporation Man** (London, 1971). It has been followed up by Keith Wilcock in his (New York, 1984) book **The Corporate Tribe**. The latter makes it quite clear that our machine society has really changed man's relationship to territory — or space. If I may quote him: 'The dramatic changes in communication and transportation make corporate man different from all his predecessors . . . machines influence almost every aspect of modern man's daily life. Automobiles, television, computers, airplanes, refrigerators, telephones, snowmobiles, microscopes, outboard engines, electric ranges, tractors, electric light bulbs, trains, wristwatches, factories bursting at the seams with drills, presses, mixers, shears and hoists, elevators, typewriters, rockets, the bomb — are all very recent additions to man's environment . . . Machines now transport man, keep him warm or cool, educate him, provide life support when he is ill, solve problems for him, help him plant, harvest, process, cook and prepare his food'.

Well, we know that much of this development is helpful,

to say the least. Nevertheless, Wilcock continues: 'The existence of machines as a ubiquitous part of our environment has the effect of changing man. Machines are changing our work, our play, our relationships, our religions, our customs, our taboos, our education and our territorial ties. They are changing war, politics, and governments'. And he goes on to say: 'The varied cultural values and religious beliefs that exist in homes are brushed aside by television programming . . . (which have) captured the air time from Mom and Dad. All who watch receive the same message laced with the same values. We learn from what we pay attention to, and TV holds much of our attention'.

Wilcock's exposition may be somewhat exaggerated, but was it not old Aristotle who said that, in order to have a genuine point received, one sometimes has to exaggerate? The truth is that the kind of thing adumbrated many years ago by observers like Drucker and Burnham has become the order of our day. Sure, socialization can and does have an essential part to play in society, but it can also be carried too far.

BUREAUCRATIZATION

This process of socialisation (the forerunner of secularization) has been better described as one of bureaucratization. In other words, the predominant socio-cultural processes that serve as vehicles or carriers for secular institutions and secular consciousness are the specific ways of thinking and acting — the techniques — of modern high-tech society. A brief outline of their impact on religion must suffice here.

An obvious manifestation of it is the extent to which Church institutions copy the ways of their secular counterparts. Many Church bureaus today are victims of 'Parkinson's Law' — multiplying staff and facilities, organizing seminars and distributing paper to an extent that makes planning the attainment of their objectives more consuming of time and space and other resources than their actual attainment.

In his **Catholicism and Modernity** (New York, 1979), Dr

James Hitchcock has drawn attention to a less noticeable manifestation. 'The struggle to enlist episcopal prestige — a usually quite uneven struggle between sophisticated and well-organized bureaucrats and naive and poorly organized lay people — involves a process which is also endemic to modern bureaucracies but has not been noticed in the Church: the use of authority to undermine authority. . ... Newer programmes in religious education, liturgy, and other sensitive areas have not triumphed, as their proponents would like us to think, because of their self-evident superiority. They have triumphed because they have been officially mandated. . ... Although proclaiming an end to blind obedience in the Church, the professionals have invoked obedience to enforce the necessity of change' (p.105).

A linked manifestation is a surfacing to a high degree, both in the objective social framework of people's religious lives and in their subjective acceptance of it, of a breaking up of received ideas. At its centre is a fragmenting in every sector of life of the traditional values which gave former society stability and assurance. By the very fact that our contemporary world is preeminently a changing and changeable one, each and all of its constitutive parts (family, State, economy, school etc.) lose what Berger and Luckmann call 'plausibility', the reason, that is, for people to take them readily for granted, to believe in them implicitly and to stick by them unshakably. They become, as is said, 'demonopolised'[7].

That such mutability is the order of the day is clear to us when we consider the volatile nature of fashion in every sphere. What car design lasts presently for more than a couple of years, to say nothing of dress styles, artistic genres, and current fads? More striking, especially to those who have to face it, is that it would now seem that the average young man or woman will, if lucky enough to find them, have to change jobs up to five times in life.

This instability has a profound influence on religion as on other sectors of life. Perhaps the easiest way to delineate that influence is to say that it has created a 'free for all' situation for religion — a situation, that is, in which religious persuasions lack the kind of social confirmation of former days, a situation, therefore, in which individuals, families and other groups are subject to a degree of uncertainty that did not formerly exist. Whereas in the pre-modern age, the plausibility element of received beliefs and attitudes was massively sustained by society as a whole, nowadays there are always those 'others', who see differently, those who not so long ago were called 'outsiders' and 'drop outs' but who today are part and parcel . of the minorities hotch-potch that is a major feature of our world. This is sometimes called pluralism, again a term that has been employed as extensively as it is vague, and indeed frequently only confusing, because there never was complete uniformity in anything amongst any people. I think that I am on record as having said somewhere that the phrase 'pluralist society' was an 'asinine' one. Perhaps I overdid things in my choice of language on that occasion, because the term 'pluralism' has come to be used and accepted in the highest quarters, including the Catholic Church. At the same time, one must remember that it does have so many meanings (a 'buzzword' one writer calls it) as to render it very difficult to understand. In France it has come to stand for multi-channel radio and television service of a kind that does not correspond with the system presently available there. But then, the French are great at coining new terms, whether in **Franglais** or otherwise. After all, it is the French too who have managed to talk about **cohabitation** when they are not referring to its original sexual meaning but rather project it into inter-parliamentary co-existence.

PLURALISM

Leaving that aside, and taking it as meaning multi-group society, pluralism has had a curious effect on religion, one which is in line with the bureaucratization of non-religious life. For one thing, it has meant that the churches have tended to gear themselves towards a kind of sellers' stance hitherto alien to them, entering the domain of competitiveness, even to the extent of resorting to gimmicks for the purpose of wooing 'business'. Hence we have the adoption of methods appropriate to the consumer society in the hope of attracting people to church by making things easier for them. Pop music and the electric guitar are but the tip of an iceberg. There is a kind of progressive calculus to the thing — from the neglect of the use of holy water to a reluctance about auricular confession. It comes to be quite serious when one hears suggestions about permitting the contraceptive pill so that some of the faithful that are drifting away might be drawn back to the Church, or about abolishing clerical celibacy so that vocations might be increased.

Another by-product of the same phenomenon is the pullulation in the Church of experts of all kinds — the religious counterparts of the planners, consultors, functionaries and facilitators that are a feature of bureaucratic society. There are no two ways about it: it is indisputably the case that for quite some time now in the Church there has been a tremendous demand for what is called 'special ministries' — for youth, liturgy, the aged, the poor, the handicapped, intellectuals, politicians: the list is endless. And while it is quite true that there is real scope for specially trained ministers in some of these spheres, we should not forget the good old general practitioner, the honest-to-God-and-man G.P., the family doctor that so many of us remember with affection. His counterpart was the P.P., as we say in Ireland, or the Pastor as they say in America. He does tend to be forgotten today.

An additional by-product of pluralism is a 'hob-nobbing' between the churches, a kind of 'buddyism' in the face of religious decline, a courtship that is itself essentially related to the world from which it has sprung. As Peter Berger has put it, inter-church cooperation for the purpose of fund-raising, lobbying with governmental and international agencies, etc., is a manifestation of the bureaucratization of religious institutions and 'lays a social-psychological foundation for "ecumenicity" . . .' Some would go so far as to say that, within this admittedly limited perspective, even ecumenical prayer meetings can easily become artificial and forced, if not a charade of unity, going through the motions that are expected — conforming to expectations. Very recently I heard on T.V. a new ditty, sung by young people, that was anything but complimentary to ecumenism.

Berger is more restrained. Notwithstanding that, he does say that ecumenicity 'in the sense of an increasingly friendly collaboration between the different religious groups engaged in the religious market (means) that religious rivals are regarded not so much as "the enemy" but as fellows with similar problems . . . But the necessity to collaborate is given by the need to rationalize competition itself in the pluralistic situation'[8]. He goes further in also saying that 'the pluralistic situation . . . has, not surprisingly, coincided with a new emphasis on the laity, in that the "age of the laity", as defined by a number of theologians, is grounded in the character of that laity as a population of consumers. In other words, the theological proposition about the role of the laity may be understood as **post hoc** legitimations of developments rooted in the infra-structure of the contemporary religious market'[9].

This is undoubtedly a one-sided, and not very theologically-informed, way of looking at the ecumenical and lay emphasis in contemporary religion, particularly that of Catholicism after Vatican II, although it has to be admitted that it has laid bare some of the 'signs of the times' which the Council itself was at pains to recognise and take into account. One would need to be more than a little ostrich-like not to see a fair amount of the post-Conciliar preoccupations of many Catholics as in some way mirroring the concerns of the contemporary secular scene: I mean an obsession about the Third World, an unbalanced attitude to poverty in general, a myopic seeking after 'personal satisfaction', 'fulfilment', 'happiness', and an exaggerated ambition for a kind of 'takeover' of the Church by the laity on their own terms.

CHURCHISM

Berger, if we may return to him again, has provided some compelling snapshots into the way the churches have formally reacted to all this. On the one hand, he says, you have an 'accomodating posture', an effort to reorganise church institutions so as provide a more relevant and therefore more viable plausibility structure. On the other hand, you have a 'resisting posture', which seeks to fall back on and revamp traditional structures in the hope that plausibility is more likely to be strengthened in that direction. These postures have come to be known by many labels — Liberal and Conservative, Radical and Reactionary, Progressive and Traditionalist.

If one delves deeper into the matter, one finds quickly enough that it really turns on the downgrading or upgrading which is given to the sacred, the transcendental element in religion. Protestantism as a whole has never been noted for leaning heavily on the place of the sacred. On the contrary, its attitude towards the meaning of the Mass, its reduction in the number of the Sacraments, its playing down of the cult of the Virgin Mary and the saints, and of praying for the dead, have all made for a divesting itself of much that was mysterious. It is because of this that secularization has been able to make such inroads into Protestantism. By and large, Catholicism has resisted secularization better by reason of its retention of many more ways whereby the sacred is mediated to its adherents. Whereas, until recently at least, Protestantism was different from Catholicism in standing for a man-centered humanising of the world, Catholicism sought to humanise it through the implications of the Incarnation, that is, by the grace of God become man. In short, whereas the former, while undoubtedly having faith in God, tended somewhat to relegate Him to an other-worldly realm, and concentrated on the immanent possibilities open to man, the latter was more orientated towards transcendence in the sesse of an all-encompassing and practised persuasion that God and his grace through Jesus Christ is absolutely necessary for the transformation of human reality.

PROTESTANT V. CATHOLIC THEOLOGY

That basic difference in outlook can be seen quite clearly between Protestant and Catholic theology until relatively recently. A slant towards immanence is what lay at the bottom of Rudolf Bultmann's effort at 'demythologization', Dietrich Bonhoeffer's 'religionless Christianity', John Robinson's 'God as Daddy in the Drawing Room', and Harvey Cox's 'Secular Religion'. Undoubtedly, it received its most challenging and far-fetched exposition from the group of theologians associated with Thomas Altizer, and known as the 'Death-of God' school[10]. Altizer managed to find considerable hearing, influenced as he was by Karl Barth's original dominance of the 'Humanity of God' approach, simply because Barth's labouring of the centrality of God's Word in history was, for all its merit, channelled through a non-trancendental system of human utterance. The ultimate in this gradual but ever more radical Protestant theology has found expression in Altizer's statement that 'traditional theology must be challenged by a theology which encounters the world — even if such confrontation condemns theology to negation of itself'. It is a statement that was exceeded, if that were possible, only by the reductionist propositions of Paul van Buren, himself a doctoral student of Barth's[11]. We need not be taken aback then when we find among the most recent collection of essays from such pens, entitled **Deconstruction and Theology** [12], one chapter headed 'The Deconstruction of God' and another 'The Being of God When God is Not Being God'!

As I have already indicated, Catholic theology does not take to this kind of thing readily. Nevertheless, the appearance of Modernism in the early twentieth century — to say nothing of the Syllabus of Errors issued by Pope Pius IX in 1864 — should have been enough to alert people to what could happen. That it did happen is evidenced by a flood of books, leaning in the direction of the Protestant theology which I have described. Hans Küng's study of the Church is among the best known [13], and it should not be forgotten either that Küng's original doctoral dissertation was on the theology of Karl Barth.

As part of this tide, too, it would be a mistake to overlook the work (for long unknown) of Teilhard de Chardin. For, in common with much of the theology that I have earlier cited, Teilhard's vision is anchored to the idea that the other world is eventually here below, arrived at through a faith that enables man to become fully man, to expand and evolve into his own human authenticity.

But if theological developments, even in the Catholic Church, can provide us with examples of the sacred being sometimes obscured by the profane, it is in the areas of everyday Christian living that one comes across the most striking clues in the same direction. Pushed by the techniques and demands of the secularly produced modern bureaucratic machine, we find supposedly religious popular magazines for children, such as Catholic scouts, copy-catting their purely secular counterparts to a point that in no way or only in a very minute way is calculated to raise the consciousness of their readers towards an ideal that transcends their day to day experience. Penance and the cross, sacrifice and suffering, sin and reparation — these ideas have, to an alarming extent, been buried in favour of the more acceptable ones of peace, liberation, justice, and so on, without being too specific either as to how these are to be attained[14]. What is sought after is the mounting of one 'happening' after another — like the Band Aid phenomenon of 1985 — without asking anything from youth that really requires sacrifice.

THE 'RELIGIOUS' LIFE

This is a fair point at which to introduce some considerations — again from a sociological viewpoint — concerning the mystery of the Religious Life and what it is up against at present. Here the bedrock problem is one of identity and (apart from certain aspects that pertain exclusively to the consecrated religious state) the problem is not altogether different from that which affects religious believers in the widest sense, that is, an identity crisis caused by the technologization, bureaucratization, pluralization and desacralization of society that have turned religious institutions and belief almost upside down in the course of a couple of generations.

As Thomas Luckmann has expressed it, there is a religious layer of individual consciousness that has a relation to personal religious identity analogous to the relation which institutional religion has to the system of ultimate relevance that legitimises adherence to it. In other words, personal religious identity normally needs the supportive framework of an 'official', 'received', 'accepted' model of an historical church, a church that is recognizable and recognised as such by everybody — through its buildings, its liturgy, its theology and catechetics, its ministers and their dress, the image which it portrays to the world. Sure, it is and always has been true that there must be some room for diversity within this picture. The official model does allow — as regards discipline and dress, some ritual expressions, and more especially popular piety — certain limited departures from the broad line. This affords room for containable elements of individual religious expression and identity, sometimes on a rather extensive scale. They call it acculturation today in the international Catholic scene, but it always has had profound application in the Church and not least in the form of the varigated religious orders that are part of our rich inheritance[15].

The difficulty in our times about preserving a secure religious identity is that people do not feel themselves part and parcel of a supportive structure as surely as their forefathers did. As somebody has said, they 'confront' events and developments rather than 'live' them calmly in common with others. Their ties with their religious environment are weakened by all that is going on in their religious institutions — partly imposed on them by their religious leaders, partly the result of their own passivity. For, even though one hears often of a resistant silent majority, in reality the silent majority (to the extent that it is silent) is a spineless entity that takes a lot of shaking up to galvanize it into action. And so, as the stability of people's religious world is shaken, so is the stability of their personal religious identity.

It should be noted, though, that the most significant occasions in which people (whether Catholic or otherwise) seem to come to terms with reality are funerals or times of terrestrial destruction, such as earthquakes or famines. Why this should be, as it undoubtedly is, ought certainly be a matter of concern to those who proclaim themselves to be 'secularists'.

MEDIA MATTERS

The whole world knows that it is dominated by the media of communication. I mean the media of 'idea communication' and not just the social communication that is made possible by automobile, train, ship or plane travel.

Even though an enormous volume of literature has been produced about the nature and effects of the media, some simple elements seem to have escaped the observers. I am referring to the way in which the presentation of ideas by the media has changed over the course of the past fifty years.

I think it is true to say that fifty years ago and even much later, journalists wrote their pieces for their newspapers in a pretty objective way. Even when they did not like in particular what they were reporting, they reported it and the reader could take it or leave it. I was reminded of this quite forcibly recently when I came across in the London **Times** some reprints of reports at the outbreak of the Spanish Civil War. By and large they were statements of fact, even though the choice of the facts reported caused some of the reporters to be transferred to other posts by their editors.

In the 60's and 70's a new genre of reporting began to come in, on the part of 'correspondents', as their sources came increasingly to be called, a reporting, which while not necessarily supressing the facts, became more and more a commentary and exposition of the reporter's views about them. The readers' thoughts were being formed for them.

At the moment a more peculiar trend is underway, the replacement of both straight reporting or commentary on events by what can only be termed essays, often facetious and school girlish. They normally make good reading but can be quite unreliable and injurious.

I think that this development deserves notice because it means that newspapers (and, for all their warts our Irish newspapers are second to none in the world as any seasoned traveller knows well) are in the process of becoming 'magazines' or 'journals'. Those who know France well are aware that the French rarely read newspapers at all (they get the news from the 'tele' or the 'rad') but swamp their homes with glossy and superficial **papiers**. Is that trend spreading? As a matter of fact, one is forced to wonder whether the new **Independent** newspaper just launched in Britain, and aimed, we are told, at the Yuppies (young, upwardly mobile professionals) will be anything other than a journalists' newspaper in the sense of being a vehicle for what up and coming journalists expect their readers to want to hear. It will be interesting to see what place religious affairs will occupy in it, or, if at all, how.

1 P. Drucker, **The Concept of the Corporation** (New York, 1946).
2 D. Bell, **The Coming of Post-Industrial Society: A Venture in Social Forecasting** (New York, 1973); also Alain Touraine, **La Societé Post-Industrielle** (Paris, 1969).
3 J. Ellul, **La Technique ou l'enjeu du siécle**,(Paris,1954): English translation: **The Technological Society** (New York, 1964); Also J. K. Galbraith, **The New Industrial State** (New York, 1967).
4 J. Burnham, **The Managerial Revolution** (New York, 1941); F. Hayek, **The Road to Serfdom** (London, 1944). Also L. von Mises, **Bureaucracy** (English translation: London, 1945), and Wm. H. Whyte, **The Organization Man** (New York, 1965).
5 Cf. David E. Lilienthal, **Big Business: A New Era** (New York, 1953).
6 Pope John XXIII, Enc. **Mater et Magistra**, 15 May, 1961.
7 Cf. P. Berger, **The Sacred Canopy**, Ch. 6.
8 Op. cit., 141.
9 Op. cit., 147.
10 Cf. Th. Altizer, op. cit.
11 Cf. P. van Buren, **The Secular Meaning of the Gospel** (New York, 1963); also R. Robertson, **The Sociological Interpretation of Religion** (Oxford, 1970), 208.
12 Carl A. Rasche, ed., **Deconstruction Theology** (New York, 1982).
13 Cf. H. Küng, **The Church** (London, 1965).
14 See Pierre Debray, **Les Technocrates de la Foi** (Paris, 1968), 87ff.
15 Th. Luckmann, op.cit., Ch. V: 'Individual Religiosity', 69-76.

4

The Privatization of Life

During the course of a visit to Dublin some time ago, I was struck by some graffiti, one of which proclaimed 'New Ideology: Low Profile'. Only a short time afterwards I came across a newspaper report of a lecture in which somebody deplored a lack of leadership in Ireland today. And while pondering over both of these utterances, I began to recall some points from various sociological sources which go to clarify what is at issue.

It takes very little reflection to realise that contemporary society is to an increasing degree marked by a privatization of life. This development is best understood by contrasting the main features of society in former times with that of the present.

The older type of society — centered on the village, the small town and the small city, predominantly non-technological and full of face to face relationships — was characterized by a high level of integration of individual and community. Sure, there were differences between people, but at the same time there was a real hanging together. There was no dichotomy between the small life-world of the individual and the life of the community as a whole. The individual knew pretty well all those whom he or she encountered in his or her daily rounds, whether neighbours, grocers or beggars. He or she could predict their actions and reactions. He or she was prepared too for ups and downs in life stemming from natural causes, such as hunger, drought and disease. He or she was prepared for anything, really, within their respective life structures.

Modern society, as already outlined in the preceding chapter, is in essence very different. It is characterized by a high level of division of labour, by specialized role performance and a diversification of loyalty claims. In place of a meaningful frame of existence within a unified totality, there has emerged a pluralization of worlds — the firm, the economy, the State, the EEC, the wider international scene, even the Church to some extent — all of which represent separate institutional spheres, each functioning according to its own laws and in one way or another dominating the life of the individual.

Confronted with his seeming inability to do anything effective in face of the many worlds in which he is caught up, it is not surprising that the modern individual suffers from a feeling of helplessness. Neither is it surprising that he should search for something to hold on to as his own, so to speak.

SIGNS OF PRIVATIZATION

In this context the only thing that is readily available is the construction of a domain of freedom, a domain which constitutes private life, a sphere unclaimed by the powers that be, in which there is freedom to choose, to decide for oneself, as regards one's time, one's home, one's body and even one's God or gods as the case may be.

This privatization of life is exemplified in an extreme way by those who are so alienated from society as to drop out of it altogether or to turn overmuch to drink or drugs, rock music or sexual kicks, prayer groups or sects — all little worlds either freely chosen or deliberately constructed by their dwellers.

In a more general way, privatization is exemplified among people by a withdrawal to a greater or lesser extent from public life, that is, from taking an active interest in the system of values and obligations which historically have been the basis of community life. Private lives are being lived to a point of completeness and exclusiveness hitherto unprecedented[1].

By and large, such is the state of Western society today. It is an affluent or relatively affluent society, aided by technology and the media, a society whose life-style is inescapably urban-type because its supports are possible only in an urban civilization, but a life-style which extends as well to the rural areas of the developed countries because urban culture as such is of a qualitative rather than a quantitative character and is spread in so many easily accessible ways, the media, as we know them, being but one among innumerable others.

Naturally, the effects of this urban culture, including the privatization of life, are felt most palpably in those countries in which runaway urbanism is to be found. They are less evident to us in Ireland by reason of the fact that the former rural and city life-styles are still partaken of by the older generation. Nevertheless, there are certain signs of privatization in Ireland too that are evident to the discerning.

A clear sign of privatization is the retreat of those who can, and that means, in the first place, the educated and better off, to the outer suburbs of cities and their surrounding villages, where the new private life-style can be cultivated. It is a shift which is slowly starving cities of cultural and entertainment facilities — cinemas, clubs and theatres disappearing for lack of patrons, and business properties being abandoned in downtown areas because they do not command rents commensurate with the cost of servicing them. The less fortunate are left in under-serviced conditions far from conducive to either personal or family well-being.

Of course, social contact cannot altogether be avoided. Still it is noticeable that the community efforts which appear in the fashionable outer suburbs tend to be forms of what one observer has called 'negative solidarity', as for example when residents band themselves together to fight the invasion of their privacy by any kind of communal or public structure that is capable of generating traffic or noise and so on. Even the erection of schools, youth centres or corporation housing estates can sometimes be opposed for that reason alone, whether consciously recognized or not. In other words, there is often a stark individualism behind a facade of mutual caring.

In these suburbs what social unity appears to exist is in fact infinitely graduated according to the incomes, debts, professional and other status of the individuals that inhabit them. It really has nothing to do with genuine belonging or true interdependence. It has everything to do with receiving what the system can give, with maintaining the private world of the individual's car, his house, his freezer, his recorded music, and, needless to say, his television. It is really a disunity, held together by private interest.

Television is a primary prop to the whole privatized universe. In front of it public events are watched passively, at a distance and through the intermediary of television personalities who themselves stand for nothing except their careers and to whom every event is but grist to the superficial programme mill.

IMPOVERISHMENT OF PUBLIC LIFE

All this privatization has made for the impoverishment of public life, particularly political life. One has but to think about it to realise that real concerns are generally expressed only at budget time. What will be its impact on petrol or liquor or industrial grants, on the PAYE sector, on farmers, on house acquisition and so forth, each sector having its own spokesmen. It is true that there is much public discussion about and demand for solutions to other pressing and important problems such as crime, the achievement of national aspirations, marital breakdown, social welfare, education, but one gets the impression, whether one likes it or not, that the bulk of this discussion is of an academic nature and masks a real indifference on the part of those who are comfortable.

I feel that it is because of this determination on the part of the 'haves' not to be disturbed in their life-style that the most noticed groups in our society are those dedicated to issues which cannot throw affluent consumerism into jeopardy. This latter cannot be, or at least is not generally seen to be, endangered by contraception, abortion or divorce, anti-blood sports, women's rights, anti-apartheid or disarmament. A check on the letter columns of the newspapers, almost any day, will show how themes like these hold the stage.

Faced with such self-interest, politicians would not be human if they were not tempted more and more to indulge in the politics of accommodation, what I have elsewhere dubbed as a kind of wheeling-dealing. There must be no rocking of the boat, no introduction of social changes such as would run against the preoccupation of individuals with their own comfort. For this reason political talk tends to be couched in terms that are generalized (growth rate, balance of payments, productivity, inflation) and not directly referable to the individual's specific fortunes.

As a result, the politician tends to lose caste, recognized by those whom he serves in this way as being involved in a deception which they themselves condone. It is an unenviable position in which to find oneself and is only compounded by promises, particularly before elections, or evasions such as assurances about monetary stability at times when currency devalution is known to be something that is possibly only around the corner. The life of the politician becomes a charade if it is seen to be inactive (even if forced by the electorate to be so) about the matters that count most for the nation. And it has to be admitted regretfully that to far too great an extent the acquisition and disbursement of affluence has indeed become the politician's **raison d'être**. It is on account of this that there is little serious difference between the main political parties, including even the Socialist and Communist parties, in any Western country at present. The fact that a common preoccupation has been thrust upon them does not alter their loss of credibility as parties with supposedly different ideologies.

A further product of all this is a temptation on the part of people not to become involved in public life at all, to keep out of politics assiduously (apart from contributing to party funds), to pass the buck to those in power and to survive to the extent that they renounce any feeling of responsibility or concern for others.

Those in power themselves can in turn be tempted to quit public life. This temptation, I believe, is stronger right now than we are aware of, not only by reason of the apathy and thanklessness of the people as a whole but also by being coupled with an insupportability of the politicians's burden, stemming from the pressure of media scrutiny, the technology of eavesdropping, the inability to be one's true self, and the challenge of well-documented and researched stances on the part of the self-interest groups who are nowadays as well if not better equipped for articulating their demands as government once was for 'frightening' them off.

REVOLT OF THE DISENCHANTED

The disengagement from political life to which I refer is already taking place in some post-industrial countries. The 'revolt' of youth is but the tip of an iceberg. Sociologists have come to know it as 'de-modernization'. The reaction of youth is very understandable. But, however understandable it may be, it is full of pitfalls. Its final consequence could be the very opposite of what it is intended to achieve, namely, 'the quiet life' — employement and security.

For, against a background of opting out on the part of the better educated and better off, two even more undesirable alternatives present themselves. One possibility is that the apathy which lies behind the opting out could spur radical elements to violent revolution. As a matter of fact, this apathy is recognised at the moment by political activists in all Western countries as the greatest obstacle to a change in the status quo. It is seen by them to be a guilty complicity in the retention of that **status quo**, which can be got rid of only by mindless violence and destruction, after which politicization can take place in the wake of the resultant destabilization. It is this kind of strategy that is at the back of many anarchist and suchlike groups both abroad and nearer home.

Another possibility to which the apathy of the citizens at large could contribute is the filling of political leadership by people from a very different background to those who have abdicated it, people who would man the machine of State in an inhuman and inflexible way, regardless. This is the road to ultimate totalitarianism.

Clearly, neither alternative would be for the good of the 'silent majority', which could be effective only if it expressed itself rather than remain silent.

LIMITED LOYALTIES

There is another aspect of the privatization of life which has not been noticed sufficiently. I refer to the decay of loyalty, as between individuals and the groups — whether big or small — of which they are part.

Without doubt, people, today as before, do ascribe to affiliations of one kind or another. As Wilcock, to whom I have referred before says, 'most modern men and women have several tribal affiliations'. It is a pity that he has had to describe these affiliations as 'tribal', but he is right, because society today has become a kind of tribal thing. Whether there is question of nation states, business organizations, political parties, or even Churches, this kind of affiliation manifests itself. But it is a shallow business despite that. The family is the core of the situation. If family relationships become shallow, when TV dominates all attention, members of homes sitting silently in a semicircle, instead of talking to one another and discussing affairs — watching and listening to others — how could any loyalty be formed above and beyond the constricted world of the spectator, who (whether consciously or unconsciously) is really a passive assistant at media presentations which form and deform his or her own personal convictions.

Wilcock is very astute about all this. He even sees the shallow relationships which characterise modern man as having something to do with his 'intimacy' with machines. He notices, for instance, that one of the reasons for our obvious reluctance to switch to cheaper and even safer modes of transport may well be attributable to our desperate need to be 'alone' at least during 'to-and-from' time. We also find ourselves, generally speaking, working with one set of people and playing with another, neither getting to know each other really well. 'Corporations, automobiles, suburbs, and freeways seal modern man into compartmentalized life styles. In the city, he associates with people who put on the corporate tribal costume every day. When they see him he is always wearing a suit and tie, playing his businessman role, talking about sales, profits, projects, reports and business problems. At the end of his eight-hour performance he returns home, changes costumes, and plays the father, neighbour or husband role. The sets change. The other actors change. Modern man lives with a series of separate and less-continuous relationships than his predecessors. By definition his relationships are more shallow'[2].

The upshot of the whole thing is that modern man has only transient attachments to specific pieces of 'space'. He has become, in fact, a new kind of nomad.

THE MODERN NOMAD

If we keep our eyes and ears open, we can discern many instances of this, instances of man trying to create his own private space. It is worth noting in this connection the place that art, drama, music etc. has in the process. The French psychologist P. Francastel, in his study of the sociology of art[3], maintains that space is, similtaneously, what human groups 'occupy' and what they see it as 'representing'. There is no 'space' outside and beyond the social comprehension of it, a comprehension which continually changes throughout history. The art of the Middle Ages, of the Renaissance, of the Impressionist period, of Cubism, Futurism or Abstract art of whatever kind, are none of them anything more nor less than multiple expressions of the same bedrock human experience, that of man's struggle with a space which he strives to dominate in order to free himself from it.

The esoteric meanings and symbolism that are part and parcel of all significant art are central to this point. Paintings, more than most other art forms, are literally a window through which is presented man's view of what he believes to exist on the other side of the 'glass'. Genuine art attempts to get beyond the exterior surface of what it depicts to an interior and — really — invisible something. Because it is that, art is one of the most powerful ways through which man thinks he can vanquish existence, space and time. Owing to the fact that works of art and literature are 'reflective' products of the human mind, and, more especially, because they are of their nature 'liberating' forces, they can and do run into trouble from time to time with totalitarian régimes which, by their own nature, cannot brook such independence. There is no need for us here to even begin to outline the many ways and times in which art found itself up against this difficulty, with régimes like that of Hitler or Stalin. Suffice it to say that it can be well documented if necessary.

It is true that, from time immemorial, art not only had its patrons but that they also made clear what they wanted. There are innumerable occurrences of that in the history of art, not only painting but also sculpture, music, and architecture. It was that that was responsible for the impregnation of the greater portion of European art with Christian persuasions. That was all right in its day — its space. Today, the scene is quite different due to the social developments that have been dealt with in this book in a number of ways. Today, l'art engagé, as the French call it, is an art in a state of revolt, of seeking to break away from traditional moulds and to give man the 'space' that he clamours for.

The products of this current spate have not, to date, been too happy. We find ourselves confronted with an 'a-art' or 'anti-art', in the name of liberation. Once again, the French have a good term for the outcome — le Poubellisme, best rendered in English as 'garbage can' stuff. And it is exactly that, even though museums and exhibitions compete among themselves for the 'privilege' of putting it on display. Fashion (being 'with it') has a lot to do with this but that is a subject in its own right (cf. René König, Sociologie de la Mode, Paris, 1969). Some of the most percipient critics do recognize it for what it is — a neurotic response to the pressures of the times — and have no hesitation in terming it 'the death of art'.

A rather intriguing aspect of this is that objects, para-objects and similar entities, have become the new gods of an artistic Pantheon that was once immeasurably different. We have already had occasion to speak about 'homo sociologicus' and 'homo economicus'. It is 'homo faber' who crows today, his song not really mellifluous. During the **jours de Mai**, Paris, 1968, one of the more rivetting aspects of the then 'revolution' was the extent and nature of the graffiti to be found all over the place. I know, because I happened to be there at the time. Only in Lisbon, some years later, was anything comparable to it to be found. One of these Parisian graffiti read simply: 'Man makes love to things', following which some 'philosophers' celebrated the arrival of a 'non-human sexual' situation! In point of fact the phrase 'making' love only goes to underline the insidious way in which the loss of the sacred has infiltrated even the 'holy' domain of human sexuality. Sex, in other words, has also become an object and so people speak of 'having sex' with somebody just as casually as they do of 'having a steak', 'having a drink' or 'having a cigarette' — all in the capacity of consumers. For an excellent discussion of the exclusion of sacredness from sex I would strongly recommend Christopher Derrick's **Sex and Sacredness** (San Francisco, 1982). It is that kind of consideration that is also central to Pope John Paul II's magisterial work **Love and Responsibility** (1960), in which he emphasized the need for men and women to love each other as persons, not just 'use' their bodies as objects. But the modern 'object' approach to sex is meaningful for all that. It says, in its own way, that modern man, the victim of machinery and the consumer society, and whether he knows it or not, is at the stage of risking a transfer of eroticism from the normal personal, sexual couple to inanimate, material, and disposable things. It is stunning, and becomes more so when one remembers the 'take over' today by computers and their equivalents. Won't it be wonderful when one's computer will suddenly say to its operator: 'I would like to make love to you!'

SELF-CENTERED ART

At the moment, things, happily, have not gone so far. But they are going far enough. In relation to art, we are faced with junk culture, a new aestheticism, which even though many people would regard it as rubbish and which it may well be, must be taken seriously as one form of contemporary social reaction to life. That means that we have no option but to recognize the place and meaning amongst us of a negative aesthetic. There are innumerable ways in which that could be delineated. I will confine myself to a few. I am thinking, in the first place, of the domain of literature in which, at a Paris exhibition of 1975, the greatest, the most beautiful, page of poetry, as conceived by the organizers, was a blank page — just that — le néant, as Sartre might well say, and which he was undoubtedly responsible for promoting . . . responsible for promoting darkness, silence, nothingness and death, all of which are a denial of being. Indeed did he not also promote suicide, the ultimate in privatization, through his philosophy of the absurd and of despair?

The tergiversations of modern art do not stop here. There has been at least one musical session in which the best symphonic rendition was, well yes, total silence. The same thing has been reflected in a certain seance in which — in the name of music — a 'composer' managed to take up four minutes and thirty-three seconds during which all that could be heard was the noises in the room in which microphones were placed. The same ideas are at the bottom of some present-day conceptualisations of the theatre, presented in certain quarters, in the name of 'a-spectacles' or 'anti-spectacles'.

This may seem a natural evolution, but it is not. It represents an alienation and negation of a special kind. Some abstract art is indeed compelling (and attractive). I am thinking, in particular, of the Museum in Basle, which contains really wonderful work, by Juan Gris, F. Leger, Braque and Picasso. But that having been said, one must hasten to add that a lot of contemporary art, such as the reshaped thrash that one so frequently finds in exhibitions, would be more appropriate to a scrap-metal yard were it not for the forcible way in which it draws our attention to the grotesque substratum of our empty society. After all the late Henry Moore tried — and very remarkably — to do something similar about the hollow nature of modern society, saying: 'The places between forms, holes in things, are always an obsession with me. Space is an element as important as what is solid and material'.

Despite some understandable and intelligent efforts, it is necessary to remind ourselves that at this moment of history, there is a curious phenomenon operating. It has to do, not least but surely, with the auto-destruction of art by good people who are impelled towards certain artistic expressions that are principally a psychological reaction (we will speak about alienation later) to the circumstances of their time. Actually, this destructivism in art is not unrelated to the 'deconstruction theology' that we also hear about. Who can deny that there have been occurrences in France during which violins, violas and pianos were 'ritually' broken in the name of art? It has been said, and rightly, that that kind of thing is a manifestation of both a fatigue and a malady.

This line of thought is continuable. One thinks of Georges Segal, whose porcelain productions — **nature mort, non en peintre mais autrement** — remove the 'objects' that he proposes even from normal human inspection. Segal is but one of those contemporary people who impose their personal vision on a restricted world that is prepared to accept it, removed from the wider judgement of people as a whole, whether or not art-wise disposed. Let us not be fooled by what is happening in parts of the art world — 'creations' of all sorts that are anything but an art that is questionable to say the least. In New York's Central Park there has been held what has been described as a 'total occultation' when an 'underground sculpture' was effected by way of a big hole and nothing more. The same thing has been done in an American desert where enormous blocks of granite were lodged in sub-soil cavities, again in the name of art. Possibly the most bizzare of these 'artistic' expressions has been that of an American artist who has managed to present us with a 'transcontinental work' made up of a line beginning with America, going on to the Sahara and later to the Indies as such, nothing being visible except through a camera lodged in a satellite. The justification — the legitimation of this business (for business it is, financial business at that) has been put forward by more than one commentator as the realisation of 'the immaterial', rejecting what we call the 'concrete'. How long, I wonder, will such privatization of art continue?[4]

The centre of it is that modern man has become trapped within a **horizontality** of 'things', inside which he is trying to 'liberate' himself, really in a vacuum, forgetting the transcendental substance of existence, including his own. It may seem strange but it is true that people today endeavour to flee from their world (art is but one example). The urge to leave one's country for a while, to embark on outside excursions and voyages is intimately related to what I have being writing about. As far as Ireland is concerned, a good example of this was afforded in an article in an Irish newspaper which made it very plain that some people find it necessary to leave this country regularly for various reasons, some social, some political[5]. I accept the sentiments therein contained. If people choose to go elsewhere for climatic reasons, why not also for any other reasons that they feel are valid for them? Who asks them to stay here if they are not satisfied with the environment, of whatever nature it may be? Should they expect the people of Ireland as a whole to change their convictions and way of life? The sun, the beaches and the culture of other places may please some people more than the pleasure that they may also get from living here, in a differently healthy society. If so, what of it? People have to make up their own minds. That is also the meaning of privatization.

One of the followers of the Berger-Luckmann outlook, the Dutch sociologist Anton Zijderveld, has probed this aspect of contemporary society. He notes that, confronted with the situation in which (owing to the changeability that they are subjected to and the different affiliations which demand of them a multitude of allegiances) modern people are compelled to give only a partial and somewhat coolly detached loyalty to any grouping or indeed to any person for that matter. Zijderveld develops the alienation that tempts people to withdraw into themselves in order to defend themselves against the coercive pressures that control them as members of classes or associations — call them trade unions, professions, political parties, or even religious groupings[6].

They do have possibilities open to them for such withdrawal. For just as the Welfare State can never catch all social casualites in its net but must leave some room for voluntary charitable effort, so too, despite its omnipresence and efficiency, modern bureaucracy leaves what Luckmann calls 'interstices', and Zijderveld 'voids', which the individual can fill up 'with his private meanings, his dreams, phantasies, explanations, and justifications' [7] and which, because they lie 'between' the institutional segments of society, escape the latter's structures and control and are experienced as alienable and free.

RELIGIOUS WITHDRAWAL

It would only be trying to escape to cloud cuckooland to think that these developments do not equally affect religious identity, even the identity of the 'religious' in the strict sense of that word as we have come to use it. Of course it does, just because religion and the Church have a human as well as a divine side. There are interstices here too into which the individual may drop in search of personal identity. The attempt of the Church to socialize everybody into any particular official line can all too easily evoke a veiled or overt protest in favour of individual patterns of priorities. This process can vary — as between generation gaps, places, the sexes, social classes, occupations, etc. But the end term for all can (in theory at least) be a 'dropping out' similar to that to which I have referred in secular society. Whenever people's institutional religious existence is felt overmuch by them to consist of largely mechanical and often rather anonymous roles, then they will begin to grope for a private religious world, in which, to use an old saying now, although in truth it has sprung from modern society, they can 'do their own thing'. In this way, personal religious identity becomes a private affair with at least an illusory sense of autonomy. And just as in secular life, this leaves the individual open to choosing, to an extent that was formerly unheard of, in the general sphere of religious life the same thing can be seen at work when autonomously motivated individuals join with other like-minded individuals who also are seeking a 'private religiosity'. Mutual self support of this type ('Sinn Féin' as the Irish might call it) is the socio-psychological undercarriage of the sects, the cults, the way-out charismatic groups, that are a primary feature of today's socialscape. Sometimes it may well be also the human underpin of an urge in old-time convents to devolve into small houses and diverse work vocations in the service of the world — 'like' clubbing with 'like' for those purposes.

THE LEGITIMATION OF DISSENT

Quite often, such devolution is indisputably justifiable, even necessary, capable of 'legitimation', to use another fairly recently invented term. It was Jurgen Habermas, in his **Legitimationsprobleme des Spätkapitalismus**, who first introduced this term into common socio-political discourse[8]. In common with writers like Gouldner and a number of others, he advances a theory of 'cognition' as being basic to it all. For Habermas all would be well if a distortion-free communication between people were attained. Alas, as he sees things, that is not possible, because the legitimation problems of modern (especially Western) society are seen as subject to the forces of domination and constraint. If he could only see it differently, Habermas would realize that constraints are of the very warp and woof of society and that a privatization that comes into conflict with this fundamental fact of life is only illusion. That is not to say that power, material strength, physical force and their equivalents are the only or the most respectable levers of human society, but they are there and they have to be reckoned with. As Richard Sennett has put it: 'Habermas's work is not so much a critique of the problem of legitimation now faced by culture as the very embodiment of this problem'[9]. One can see this, as Sennett points out compellingly, in the decline of the influence of the family (referring in that context to the work of Phillippe Ariès[10]). The centrepoint is that when Ariès and those who agree with him — and they are many — speak about the family withdrawing from the world in a real sense, they are accepting the reality of a world in which an attempt at a privatized family is about the only thing left, 'but it is an attempt which constantly fails because the alien world organizes life within the house as much as without it'[11]. The dangers to religion inherent in such attempts should be obvious if they are linked with a response on the part of religion and the religious life to the institutional Church. What I mean is the just as secular bodies are tempted to isolate themselves — through privatization — from the constraints of modern bureaucratization, so too religious bodies can be tempted to privatize as far as the Church is concerned[12]. Anomalously that can only mean in their case a degree of withdrawal from the structures of the Church towards those of society outside it, and in many cases that means getting involved to a greater extent with the desacralized secular society.

By all means, religion and the religious life must endeavour to insert itself into the world rather than segregate itself entirely from it. That was the message of Vatican II's **Constitution on the Church in the Modern World**[13]. Still, the correlative has a similar validity, namely, that the secular and humanistic and imitative activities of the Church could be found counterproductive to religion and the religious life if the specificity which is inextricably linked with the sacred, the mysterious, in religion were to be lost. It should not be necessary to recall the epoch-making work in this sphere of thinkers such as William James, in his **The Varieties of Religious Experience**[14] or Mircea Eliade in his **The Sacred and the**

Profane[15] to be assured that non-sacral operations on the part of the Church, while they can have some place, must not be allowed to overshadow the sacral.

There is a further aspect of the privatization of life that manifests itself progressively. I mean the independence of the private religious conscience. Max Weber described what I am getting at as an 'inner worldliness' and Thomas Luckmann as an 'inner secularization'. In Ireland for some time now we have had many examples of it. We find it reflected in letters to the newspapers, utterances of some politicians and doctors, and sometimes even in the relations of priest and bishop. In general, what is being advanced is the view that conscience is a kind of independent entity which, on the part of Catholics, is not bound to be guided by the Church.

Let me, therefore, briefly expound the meaning of conscience for the Catholic, as understood by the Second Vatican Council and addresses thereon by the Pope.

CONSCIENCE

The Council's basic position, expressed in a number of documents, is that people have a right and duty to follow their consciences. As the **Declaration on Religious Liberty** puts it: 'Everybody has the duty and consequently the right to seek the truth in religious matters so that, through the use of appropriate means, he may prudently form judgements of conscience which are sincere and true'.

At the same time, the Council is equally emphatic that the appropriate means to be used in order to ensure that judgements of conscience are sincere and true is not, as it were, just looking into one's heart, but rather the seeking of guidance from norms that are outside one's subjective tendencies. The **Constitution on the Church in the Modern World** says that in man's search for the right solution to so many moral problems which arise both in the lives of individuals and from social relationships, 'the more a correct conscience prevails, the more do persons and groups turn aside from blind choice and try to be guided by the objective standards of moral conduct'. That is what it says — 'be guided by the objective standards of moral conduct'.

The same is repeated by the **Decree on the Means of Social Communication** which emphasises that 'the Council proclaims that all must accept the absolute primacy of the objective moral order'. In other words, in making up one's mind about what is right or wrong for one in any sphere of activity that raises a question of morality, one is bound to try to find out by looking outside oneself to what the moral law lays down.

It is here that confusion is often introduced to the effect that moral matters are one thing but social, political and even professional affairs something else, to be established exclusively by different standards. The Council entirely rejects this view.

For example, the **Dogmatic Constitution on the Church** while it does indeed recognise that the world of secular affairs is governed by its own principles, is equally definite that Catholics should endeavour to take their Catholic principles also into account when acting in the secular domain. It says: 'The faithful should learn to distinguish carefully between the rights and the duties which they have as belonging to the Church and those which fall to them as members of the human society. They will strive to unite the two harmoniously, remembering that in every temporal affair they are to be guided by a Christian conscience, since not even in temporal business may any human activity be withdrawn from God's dominion'.

Likewise, the **Decree on the Apostolate of the Laity** emphasises that the spiritual and temporal spheres while distinct are so closely linked that, to use its own words: 'the layman, at one and the same time a believer and a citizen of the world, has only a single conscience; it is by this that he must be guided continually in both domains'.

All this teaching of Vatican II about conscience has been underlined by Pope John Paul II on many occasions. In his commentary on the conciliar documents, entitled **Sources of Renewal**, written in 1972 before he became Pope, he went so far as to say that the key problem of life as actually lived by

Christians is that of the link between faith and morals and that the enrichment of faith implies the formation of conscience.

He has returned to the question of conscience on many occasions since as Pope. He is particularly concerned as to where conscience is to find those guidelines outside itself which enable it to make right judgements. He frequently repeats the teaching of the Council that, to use his own words from an audience of 1983, 'moral conscience is not an autonomous judge of our actions. It derives the criteria for its judgements from that "eternal" objective and universal divine law . . . of which the conciliar text speaks'.

And he goes on: 'If moral conscience is not the ultimate instance which decides what is good and what is evil, but must conform itself to the unchangeable truth of the moral law, then it follows that conscience is not an infallible judge: it can err. . . . The consequence which derives from such an error is very serious: when a man follows his own erroneous conscience his action is no longer correct'. He admits that, if a person is unavoidably ignorant of what is really the right thing to do, he is not guilty of anything, but he would need to be very careful.

And so, the Pope goes on: 'It is not sufficient, therefore, to say to man: "always follow your conscience". It is necessary to add immediately and always: "ask yourself if your conscience is telling you the truth" . . . It is necessary to "form" one's own conscience. In that commitment the believer knows that he has a particular help in the doctrine of the Church'.

MORAL RELATIVISM

There we have it all. Conscience is not a law unto itself and for the Catholic the teaching of the Church is a safe guide. It is a teaching that can be delivered in some cases by the Pope himself, or all bishops in communion with him. But at times it can find expression in the pronouncements of episcopal conferences or even individual bishops. For the individual to neglect this teaching is to go the way of moral relativism.

73

Everybody knows for himself or herself that following one's conscience in the right way can sometimes be an agonizing thing, involving inner conflicts, hesitations caused by social pressures, temptations to elude it in the name of reasons of State, party, self-interest, and so forth. Nevertheless, the surmounting of such temptations is the great challenge that confronts the Christian in every walk of life.

It is not surprising to find the Pope, again and again, putting this before us, as well as the duty of bishops to help the faithful to form and develop a correct ethical conscience.

In 1979 he complimented Italian Catholic doctors for the exemplary witness which they bore by a timely and united adherence to the indications of the Hierarchy in the matter of a proposed legislative change in favour of abortion. In 1980 he put before Catholic school teachers their special responsibility as such. In 1981 he urged workers to keep their Catholic principles staunchly in the world of work. In 1982 he pleaded at an international gathering that Christian technologists seek to harmonize conscientiously their work and their faith.

Naturally, the same goes for politicians. In 1981, on the occasion of the centenary of the birth of a famous Italian statesman, the Pope took the opportunity to praise the testimony to his faith which a believing Catholic can make in the service of public life, by seeking to promote the common good without falling into moral relativism. He pointed out to his politician audience that a democratic State, based on the free consent of its citizens, will achieve its common good only if there is, in support of its institutions and laws, a strong moral sense and a determination to promote sound ethical values, both on the part of the citizens and those who legitimately represent them.

In that connection, I could not but be disappointed at the attitude of some politicians towards conscience that has found expression in views, if reported properly, such as: 'My conscience as a legislator is informed by what I believe to be good and necessary for this State of which I am a Minister'.

The same is true of statements such as 'I am a non-denominational politican'.

What if a decision that seems advantageous from the political viewpoint is, on moral grounds, open to objection? Could this mean that in forming one's conscience as a legislator one need not pay attention to the requirements of the moral law? Has a Catholic the right, contrary to the teaching of the Vatican Council which I have cited concerning the single, indivisible conscience of the Catholic, to distinguish between his conscience as a legislator and his conscience as a Catholic? How could he believe that what is in the interest of the State from a worldly viewpoint is thereby necessarily morally right, if it contravenes the plan of God regarding the human person or regarding the family?

As regards this, the Church has the right and duty to teach, whether the context be politics, medicine, business or any other area of life. The teaching of the Church is simply to set forth and apply the law of God, not to promote the interests of Catholics as a religious group as such. The Church has no power, no authority, to bend the law of God; it may not, even in the smallest degree, interpret that law in any interest whatsoever other than that of the truth itself which it has been commissioned to proclaim. To do so would also be moral relativism.

Catholic politicians no less than Catholics in other walks of life must take account of such teaching. And if, after doing this, a politician finds that he or she does not agree with the Church on some point, they will have to reply to the question 'Did you know that the Church taught such and such?' with the answer, 'Yes, I did, but I did not go along with it'.

It is not to be wondered at that the Church should find such an attitude disquieting. For the Church is concerned, not only with expressing its teaching in any particular domain, but in having it treated seriously with the authority which that teaching claims, according to the particular way in which it is expressed.

As I shall outline in detail in the next chapter, every

democracy depends for its moral legitimation on the moral concern of those who support it. As the American commentator Richard J. Neuhaus has put it, one enters the democratic arena as a moral actor[16]. To maintain that moral judgement must be set aside before entering political life, would not only constrict anybody's role in respect of socio-moral legitimation but, in the case of Catholics, conduce to a divided self, better known as schizophrenia. We shall see too that democracy cannot survive such 'bilateralism'. It leads inescapably to the creation of a situation into which ideologies and values other than those which the individual may privately hold come in and 'rule the roost'. Politics cannot ignore moral attitudes because the matters with which it deals so often have to do with what is right or wrong.

In this connection, Neuhaus supplies a philosophical thesis that is the analogue of the theological one regarding the conscience of the politician. In public life, he says, we need to be guided by something more than private persuasion. 'By divesting ourselves of authoritative moral referents that are external to ourselves, such as religion proposes, we have acquiesced in the judgement that there is no moral appeal beyond the individualistic pursuit of interests. I have referred to this view of the political actor as one that turns him into a cipher. It frequently happens in the modern world that another word for cipher is "citizen" (in some societies "comrade")'[17].

Granted the moral dimension of politics, it is nevertheless not for governments to manufacture and market moral visions. That is primarily the business of other institutions in society. Though one does come across examples of it, moral crusading as such is not the business of the politician. There is an important distinction — and one that should be upheld by democracy — between government and culture, of which religion is the morality-bearing part. French culture has suffered from a Ministry of Culture that has straight-jacketted it in many ways, ranging from television programmes to art. Imagine 'bourgeois' paintings being removed from display in museums under President Mitterand's government and consigned to the storerooms, to be replaced by 'revolutionary' 19th and 20th century evocations of the struggles of the working class. Art of every kind (especially theatre) can indeed be abused at the service of ideology. Everybody knows of the extent to which the Third Reich and the U.S.S.R. at one period in particular, suppressed all art of which they did not approve. Likewise in some Eastern European countries, the Churches have not really benefitted from the existence of Ministries of Religion. Prescinding from all political frameworks, it is not for government personnel as such to lecture on the ecclesiastical law of Church-State relations, or themes proper to dogmatic or moral theology.

To come back: Privatization is in a very real sense **the** enemy of religion in our day. Niklas Luhmann (not to be confused with Thomas Luckmann), in his book **The Function of Religion**, actually defines secularization as 'the social-structural relevance of the privatizing of religious decision'[18]. In other words, he regards the new subjective attitude to religion as **the** sign of a secular society in which on the whole 'religion is no longer functionally necessary but is only summoned to be "helpful" in certain situations'. I think we know what he means. No wonder Michael Harrington should have titled his book (published in New York in 1983) **The Politics at God's Funeral**[19]. Harrington himself accepts that the 'Political Theology' that is so much a feature of some segments of today's 'Christendom' recognizes, to quote him directly, that 'privatization is the great enemy of religion in the modern world — not, as some sociologists think, its salvation'.

Perhaps those who 'indulge' in privatization — in the name of personal freedom — should remember what Zijderveld says, speaking of the 'voids', as he puts it (I would prefer to say 'mouseholes'), that today's society gives to people to 'opt out': 'The individual calls this his private autonomy, or even "freedom", but is unaware of the fact that this "freedom" is merely **residual**: it is, so to speak, put together from the leftovers of a segmented social structure. These leftovers are embellished with uncommitted feelings, sentiments, and irrationalities. The intellectual style is made up of free-floating impressions. With Luckmann, one might call this "freedom" largely illusory'[20].

Catholic politicians, more than others, should take a hard look at these matters and not allow themselves to be seduced into the new religion of politics that prevails in so many countries. For there is no denying that a purely secularist concept of politics is being widely followed today. And once politics is understood to be independent of religion, it is soon rendered well nigh sacred itself.

Dr James Hitchcock of St Louis University has put 'no tooth' on the facts when he writes: 'It is no exaggeration to say that for many contemporary Christians political activity — walking picket lines, making speeches, drafting platforms, campaigning on behalf of favoured candidates — has taken on a sacred meaning, has become in effect a new liturgy, far more meaningful than the old liturgy. . ... (Many Catholics) will tolerate, and even embrace, in the name of a more perfect social order, conditions and ideas which they have already rejected in the Church itself. In politics they are prepared to surrender their personal freedom, their autonomy, in the name of a higher good. They deem it a privilege to be asked to give themselves totally to the cause, even as they are condemning such dedication in religion.'[21]. And again: 'For many Christians political activity now has sacramental value and serves as a surrogate religion. In 1972, for example, a former Jesuit priest, writing in the Catholic press, asserted that the Democratic Party convention in Miami Beach was a true gathering of the people of God, more so than any church. The convention's orators were compared to biblical prophets and their orations characterized as "the power of the sermon momentarily revived"'. Truly, politics has in certain respects taken the place of religion for some.

It is for this reason that one can find Catholics promoting, in the name of a better social scene, ideas and measures that are not accepted by the Church. Only something such as this can explain the messianic zeal with which some give themselves up to advancing the cause of contraception, divorce and the like. Unless this fanatical politics is checked, by the end of the century all over the Western and so-called Christian world genuinely Catholic social expression will have been pushed out of most areas in the interests of what legislators regard as more important political goals.

Catholic politicians should be on their guard against this, for I am sure that, deep down, they would hardly want it thus. On the contrary, they should be giving strong and unequivical leadership as Catholic politicians. They should realize that, as leaders and, in fact, an élite, even more is expected of them in this respect than of the rank and file of those who support them. As an élite, they are called by the Church not to limit themselves to the minimum requirements of the Church but to do more. In this way, they could help to combat the process of de-Christianization which has overtaken the Western world.

THE ALIENATION FACTOR

Not alone politicians, but all Catholics who choose to follow political party whips irrespective of what the Church might say, categorically have a problem on their hands — that of reconciling their Catholic convictions with the directives (no, that is the wrong word; rather should I say teaching authority) of their Bishops and the duty of the Bishops themselves to stand by that.

Unless Catholics are careful in this respect, they could easily become alienated in a way that leads to anti-clericalism. Privatization of the individual conscience, if carried too far, can cause tensions and even a kind of psychosis that leads to the alienation that I am talking about. Talcott Parsons used to say, in his earlier writing, that civilized society, while imposing constraints on the individual by way of codes of law and the like, also enters directly into his consciousness by an internal, psychological process which ensures that his conduct is self-imposed as well. In other words, social norms are constitutive rather than merely regulative of human behaviour. As a consequence, the individual who freely and consciously violates these internalized norms is bothered because of a feeling that he has failed to respect what he believes.

Later propositions, derived mainly from Freudian psychology, maintained that the superego, as it has been termed, does not operate in that way at all. In fact, it came to be accepted by many scholars that guilt feelings are more common amongst people who do try to conform to norms which they have genuinely internalized and who do not consciously violate their private moral code, which they accept yet question for one reason or another and generate a frustration within themselves. A not unusual way in which such people seek to purge themselves of this frustration is by self-persuasion that, after all, they are being asked to live up to what is really impossible. And when they do not conform their behaviour to what is expected by their code — whether secular or religious — they seek to avoid guilt by repressing any consciousness of failure. The stance of some Catholics in respect of the teaching of **Humanae Vitae** is a prime candidate for that kind of process.

Latter-day sociologists are inclined to take a broader and more complex view of these matters — 'deviant behaviour' if one wants to categorise scientifically. They tend to recognize that the relations between social norms and the individual's selection from among them, his conduct and even his feelings about it, are neither self-evident nor easily understood. Far from causing a guilt syndrome, the result can be a free-wheeling in a tenaciously privatized consciousness in which internal conviction becomes a norm in itself, minimalizing any external pressures other than those to which the individual himself is prepared to conform. Conformity, even to the norms which he 'secretly' adheres to, becomes irrelevant. Outwardly he does one thing, inwardly he may think differently[22].

ACCEPTANCE SEEKING

But a difficulty remains, just because men and women are so built that they are 'acceptance seekers', profoundly sensitive to the expectations of others, in every domain of life. Ralph Linton has put it very plainly when he says that 'the need for eliciting favourable responses from others is an almost constant component of personality. Indeed, it is not too much to say that there is very little organized human behaviour which is not directed toward its satisfaction in at least some degree'[23]. It is true that sociologists can and often do overestimate the role of social pressures on the individual. One has to remember Dahrendorf's caution about that. Nevertheless, it is a fact that there are immensely powerful socializing factors in human behaviour. As has often been said: 'No man is an island'. One notable contemporary sociologist has spoken about 'the intensity with which men desire and strive for the good opinion of their immediate associates in a variety of situations, particularly those where received theories or ideologies have unduly emphasized other motives such as financial gain, commitment to ideals, or the effects on energies and aspirations of arduous physical conditions'. Thus sociologists have shown that factory workers are more sensitive to the attitudes of their fellow-workers than to purely economic incentives; that voters are more influenced by the preferences of their relatives and friends than by campaign debates on the 'issues'; that soldiers, whatever their ideological commitment to their nation's cause, fight more bravely when their platoons are intact and they stand side by side with their 'buddies'[24].

Pace Dahrendorf, there is no denying that much of this is so. People do cultivate their own reference groups and circles of significant others. It holds for trade unions, for politicians, for journalists, for businessmen, for Church-goers. And it is not to be condemned. It is human nature. A problem arises only when such groups so self-validate themselves as to lose contact with society as a whole, whether in Church or State. Naturally, this book is particularly concerned with groups — Catholic groups — who place economic or nationalistic or political party affiliations before their religious loyalties if not credences. That such can happen should be obvious.

ANTI-CLERICALISM

The arrival of a real (even if often subdued and even cloaked) anti-clericalism is a major effect of this where the Church is concerned. Strangely enough the word 'anti-clericalism' is of more or less recent vintage, having appeared in France about 1850 but whose usage blossomed between then and 1870. Its roots are ancient, however. Indeed it is as old as the Church itself. Interestingly enough, it is a Catholic thing to the extent that historically it has flourished mainly where Catholicism exists (with due allowance, of course, for a less pronounced Protestant version of it). Its origins were certainly in Catholic countries. Many histories of it have been written, one of the most recent and best being René Remond's **L'Anticlericalisme en France, de 1815 a nos jours**[25]. It becomes clear that it is caused by many factors — from the charge that the Church is too interested in money, to clerical scandals, whether true or false, to the accusation against monks for being 'lazy', the supposed 'deviousness' of the Jesuits, suspicion of a 'liberal' Church by its right wing followers, the venom of the left on the other side, jealousy of an alleged 'domination' by the Church of education and hospitals, and, needless to say, particular cases and episodes such as that of Dreyfus and that of Canon Kir, the priest who, as Deputy Mayor of Dijon, sought to receive Nikita Khrushchev but was prevented from doing so by episcopal intervention — or so it was asserted. In recent times all that kind of thing is being chronicled by magazines such as **Le Canard enchainé** in France and similar ones elsewhere, not all of them as obviously prejudiced as it is.

Despite all that, it is Remond's conviction that the real basis of anti-clericalism is a reaction to the Church's claim to guide consciences especially in political affairs or rather politico-moral affairs. It is not, he says, just a negative reaction to circumstances. While not an appendage of any particular social group, it is for all that a political ideology, resting not on abstract ideas but on a kind of fear of the Church, and resentment too, in short, on emotional and affective grounds. It has provided in many places a perfect alibi, more often than not at the hands of the bourgeois left, for playing a decisive part in political struggles. Cardinal Ratzinger in his book **The Ratzinger Report**[26], has referred in a different yet not unrelated context to those contemporary bourgeois loyal dissenters who seek to impose their own structures on the Church itself.

Anti-clericalism pertains to the relationship between the faith of individuals and their actual comportment in society and Church, more especially in what concerns ecclesial v. civil society. It is an extreme interpretation of 'Render to Caesar the things that are Caesar's and to God the things that are God's'. Whereas the Koran refuses to separate these, the anti-clerical would drive a coach and four between them. He thus proceeds both as one who is affiliated to Christianity yet reacts violently to its historical application of the Gospel in the civil domain. Even when there is a thoroughly necessary breach made by Church authority in the invisible frontier between ecclesial and civil society, the anti-clerical will object **in the name of personal liberty**. It is for this reason that it is part and parcel of a privatization which, in the religious field, would separate the sacred and the profane, religion and secular life. True, since Vatican II, it has had to adapt its postures to the new face presented to it by the Council documents, but it has done so only by trying to use this for its own purpose, which is an uncompromising privatization of religion and life.

The subject of anti-clericalism has come up, naturally and inevitably, out of the discussion which we have been conducting in the previous pages. But 'anti' is something that has a wide application and, before I finish this chapter, I would like to engage in one aside related to it, that is, the contemporary 'anti' attitudes of so many young people in relation to so many things.

Goodness knows, it is hard to blame them and I do not propose to do that. It is so difficult for so many of them to find jobs and even for the best qualified amongst them to succeed in following their chosen careers. It has reached a point which everybody should be aware holds out real possibilities of social cataclysm.

THE 'OPTION' FOR REVOLUTION

In the sixties and early seventies we saw something similar in France, at the end of May 1968 in particular, when both students and professors, pupils and teachers in many parts of that country but especially in Paris united in combating what they regarded as a system which refused to accord to them that degree of participation in the direction of their affairs which they felt was their right. It was a movement that was only put down by the use of force.

But, in truth, it was more than a movement. It was a 'revolution' in a real sense of that term, a revolution which — ironically — stemmed from the wealth and prosperity of that particular period. Indeed it was, as is said, a 'biting of the hand that fed them' on the part of those involved — a syndrome by no means unknown before. At the same time and for the same reasons, you had in England and the United States of America analagous revolutions on the part of students and staffs in the majority of third-level educational institutions, revolutions that shook the very foundations of those institutions both in the redbrick and the ivy league.

It was the same kind of thing that was responsible for the appearance during those decades of the 'beatniks', the 'flower children', the 'teddy boys', the 'skin-heads', the motor cycle 'Hell's Angels', and the 'provos', — whether they originated in Liverpool or Manchester or London, San Francisco or Amsterdam — nearly all of which categories came from upper-class or middle-class grades of society. Indeed it would appear that their **fons et origo** was a 'rage' (I use the word in its pure etymological sense) against the very affluence of the consumer society that had liberated them from dependence on anybody in the matter of 'getting on' in the world. Indeed so easy was it to get jobs at that time that some people like self-dubbed 'On the Road' Jack Kerouac just moved from one job to another as and when they liked and celebrated their restlessness, their rootlessness, their creepiness, in song. It was a world of rock and roll. They could afford to get away from it all whenever they wished. One recalls **Easy Rider** and **The Yellow Submarine**. Both figuratively and literally, it was the era of the 'Rolling Stones', the 'Beatles', and the 'Bay City Rollers'.

I have personal reason to remember those years because in the Summer of 1969 I gave a series of lectures in the University of San Francisco where the 'beautiful people' of Haight Ashbury were still to be found, although many of them had by then moved out of town up into the mountains, to such places as Grass Valley, where I actually visited some of them, saw something of their ways and found out something about the motives which prompted them. I have written about this at length in my book entitled **Conscience versus Law**, published in Dublin in 1970.

CONTRASTS: YESTERDAY AND TODAY

What a difference today! Gone is the irresponsibility of youth or, gone it is to an extraordinarily high degree — apart of course from the intended to shock, rainbow hairdos of the punks, the stamping of the boot boys and the abrasivness of the leather and studs brigade. In a real sense it is not a good tendency, because whatever one might say about the flower children or even the hippies, they had something in them of a **joie de vivre** which the present rebellious do not. Rather, when they are not in fact ominously threatening in their demeanour, the dissatisfied youth of today is coldly aggressive, harbouring a deep resentment against the generation that bred them and (one sometimes cannot but feel) almost prepared for the possibility of open revolt against the system within which they find themselves.

For the present, that has been staved off in various ways —

youngsters getting their kicks by way of barbarism at football fixtures, letting off steam at frenzied discos and stabbing each other betimes on the way home. It is true that this scene that I have painted is an extreme picture and a very very exaggerated one and for that one can only be thankful. At the same time it could very easily boil over into kicking in the shop window displays of the **societé de consommation** and the rolling of the heads of the wealthy if not exactly after the manner of the French Revolution.

Naturally, in such situations, reactions vary according to different countries and the different strata of society. Youth from the more upper-class drawers go in for more sophisticated sulking than their less privileged counterparts. And there is still, thank God, especially in those countries in which Catholicism continues to be strong, Ireland included, a tremendous generosity and vitality and flexibility amongst youth which is prepared to put up with an awful lot in the hope of better things to come and would die rather than debase itself.

As regards the revolt of intellectuals in today's world, there is a new feature which was not there to any great degree before now and that is a solidarity between students and their academic staffs in the very matter of revolt. As I have said, it was to be found to some extent in Nanterre during the Paris revolution of May 1968, as well as in the British and American (and also indeed the Irish) student revolutions of the late 60's and early 70's. But there is another striking difference between the temptations to 'kick the bucket' that haunted the students of yester-year as against those that beset students and teachers today, i.e., and that is that, whereas the earlier temptations were fomented by a taking of things for granted while nurturing a thanklessness — indeed a Freudian complex — towards the way of life that had produced and pampered them, today's dissident members of the family and the nation are spurred in inverse fashion by an anger that 'in no way' is enough being done for them by the received or established society. Whereas previously they took, with unbelievable casualness, what home and government gave to them, yet still dropped out by way of showing their independence of the system, now they tend to drop out (and not necessarily by removing themselves to another habitat) for the purpose of showing that they feel they are being let down. 'You owe me' is the phrase most commonly heard today from their children by parents in the average American family.

Of course, the matter does not stop with the family. In fact it is fraught with important consequences for government. A first consequence is a demand on government for jobs and for that matter a demand on the Church too for jobs as if the latter were in any significant position to do anything directly about that. A second consequence is a tendency on the part of government — as governments tend to do what comes naturally to them anyhow — to defend what they are doing or failing to do. The result is the gradual emergence of a confrontation between not just the haves and the have-nots but between youth in general and the society that has produced it. It involves a contradiction in the classical sense, the kind of contradiction which in a Marxist orientated, or should I say a predominantly materialistically orientated society, could easily erupt into a full-grown Marxist revolution but which in Western Liberal Democracies (to a considerable extent owing to the Christian heritage which they still possess) is still contained.

· What is tending to happen in the West is the making of a distinction by the dissatisfied between Marxist Ideology and Marxist Analysis, the former purely materialistic and anti-religious and abhorrent to the majority of the youth, but the latter gaining acceptance for the thesis that the only way forward towards the achievement of social justice is by way of class conflict of one kind or another. This approach is not confined to youth nor is it confined to secular interests. I have seen it expressed obliquely in a couple of publications that have appeared in Ireland, one contributed to by priests and both male and female religious, and the other, whose title voiced its concern for the creation of what it called 'an Irish Theology', and contributed to by priests, religious and lay people. This kind of diluted liberation of theology is probably the most difficult philosophico-theological problem that Catholic intellectuals (and particularly the younger amongst same) have to contend with today. It is not for us here to get involved in the pros and cons of debate about it. My purpose in introducing it is simply to underline the fact that it does have a connection with the considerations that I started out with, namely, the dissillusionment of so many young people today (and notably young teachers) with the socio-economic system. I say 'notably' young teachers, because it is of the very nature of their training and function as teachers to seek to conscientize society

THE SYSTEM FIGHTS BACK

One of the ways in which the system fights back in face of these present discontents is through the development of training programmes whose ostensible object is to inculcate moral values part of whose object is to get young people to fit in with government aims. This approach, which began in the United States, has now been adopted widely elsewhere and is part of the H.E.B. programme for schools in Ireland. Its results have come to be very controverted in America and at present there is quite a lot of discussion about it too in Ireland. Rightly so, because it is well to be aware of the possible ambit and effects of any such programme, the extent to which it could weaken traditional moral directives and replace them with value-free suggestions for conduct or at most simple norms of civics. Similar processes are being introduced and experimented with all over the place. At present in Britain there is quite a controversy about books used by the Inner London Educational Authority which are said to re-write history along party-political lines.

All such attempts at imposing moral and even thought control on people is surely something to be viewed with great concern. Otherwise a moral and social upheaval of unimaginable extent could be just over the horizon — a Rambo-type world of the film **New York 2000**.

The reasons for the need to be aware of this are many. One of them is that, unless one is conscious of its existence it cannot be averted at all and, secondly, as far as revolt on the part of youth is a specific aspect of today's alienation against the Church in many places, it is largely a reflection of what is going on in secular society and not just an exclusively religious problem.

It is worth noting, though, that the attitudes of youth can be very different in different contexts and given different expectations. The plight of youth in the Third World, desperate though it is, does not lead as quickly and explosively to radical violence as that of those who live in a still relatively comfortable society. Even the structures of their satisfactions can change. Twenty to thirty years ago, the 'small is beautiful' motto was everything. Today, while it still does have its importance, there is a new hankering after 'big happenings' — large youth gatherings that give a sense of togetherness and belonging, whether on the international scene such as the Olympic Games or Papal Masses or on the domestic fronts of Croke Park and Slane.

Cultural differences like these could provide pastoral opportunities of which the Church was formerly unaware. Today, for example, would mini-churches, little groups with their guitars etc., be the ideal framework for general communal worship? Or is it not the case that youth today get more confidence from seeing others also worshipping — others of all ages, groups and classes?

Privatization may have had its day.

1 M. Pawley, **The Private Future** (London, 1923); also Peter L. Berger, **Facing up to Modernity** (New York, 1977).
2 K. D. Wilcock, **The Corporate Tribe** (New York, 1984), pp. 72-73.
3 P. Francastel, **Études de Sociologie de l'art** (Paris, 1970).
4 For much of this exposition I am indebted to the little known but important work of Jean Brun, **Les Vagabonds de l'occident** (Paris, 1976).
5 Cf. Douglas Kennedy, 'An Outsider Looking in', in **The Irish Independent**, 16 August, 1986.

6 Cf. A. Zijderveld, **The Abstract Society: A Cultural Analysis of Our Time** (New York, 1970), Ch. 5 'Autonomy in Pluralistic Society', pp. 125-139.

7 Zijderveld, op.cit., p.135.

8 English translation, **Legitimation Crises** (London, 1976).

9 Cf. R. Sennett, 'Destructive Gemeinschaft', in ed. Bocock et al., **An Introduction to Sociology** (London, 1980). See also Sennett, **The Fall of Public Man** (New York, 1978).

10 E.g. in **Sexualités Occidentales**.

11 Sennett, loc. cit.., p. 109.

12 Gianfranco Poggi, 'State and Society under Liberalism and after', in Bocock et al., op.cit.

13 Vatican II, Past.Const. **Gaudium et Spes**.

14 First published in 1902.

15 M. Eliade, **Le Sacré et le Profane** (Paris, 1965).

16 Richard John Neuhaus, **The Naked Public Square: Religion and Democracy in America** (Grand Rapids, 1984), p.125.

17 Op. cit., p.126.

18 N. Luhmann, **Funktion der Religion** (Frankfurt-am-Main), 1977.

19 M. Harrington, **The Politics at God's Funeral: The Spiritual Crisis of Western Civilization** (New York, 1970)

20 A. Zijderveld, **The Abstract Society** (New York, 1970), p.135.

21 J. Hitchcock, 'The New Religion of Politics', in **L'Osservatore Romano**, 28 September, 1978. Cf also Hitchcock, **Catholicism and Modernity** (New York, 1979), Ch.8 — 'The Kingdom of Politics'.

22 Cf. Dennis H. Wrong, 'The oversocialized conception of man in modern sociology', in an **Introduction to Sociology** (London, 1980).

23 R. Linton, **The Cultural Background of Personality** (New York, 1945), p.91.

24 D. H. Wrong, op.cit., p.32.

25 Paris, 1976.

26 **Rapporto Sulla Fede** (Milan, 1985); English translation: Leominster, 1985.

5

The Emergence of Civil Religion

The developments which we have been dealing with in the last two chapters have given rise to a further — and until recently little recognized — social phenomenon of grave importance for religion as commonly understood. I refer to the emergence of what is called 'civil religion'.

As far back as 1963, Luckmann had spotted the possibility of this when he wrote: 'What are usually taken as symptoms of the decline of traditional Christianity may be symptoms of a more revolutionary change: the replacement of the institutional specialization of religion by a new social form of religion. One thing we may assert with confidence: The norms of traditional religious institutions — as congealed in an "official" or formerly "official" model of religion — cannot serve as a yardstick for assessing religion in contemporary society. . ... What is the hierarchy of significance in the world views of contemporary industrial societies? Is that hierarchy articulated in a sacred cosmos and, if so, how distinct and consistent is this articulation? What are the nature and the origin of the religious representations that constitute the sacred cosmos? What is their basis in the social structure?'[1]

Luckmann was wondering whether there is such a thing as 'modern' religion, as he termed it, and whether it has any institutional social form comparable to 'traditional' religion? Needless to say, he was speculating against the background of modern secularism and probing its most profound possible effects. He was not speaking at all about religion based on faith in supernaturally revealed truths. Rather he was making the hypothesis that religion in that sense, far from finding its inherited reflection in the developed societies, may well be in process of being challenged, if not ousted, by some new system, about which he was vague but which somehow might qualify for being called 'religion'.

THE FUTURE OF RELIGION

There is no doubt, of course, but that he raised a meaningful question. For in a largely secularized society, one has to raise questions about the future of religion. Can one assume, ostrich-like, that traditional-type religion, and, in particular, Christianity (Catholic Christianity especially) will ultimately prove immune to the present social cataclysm? Is it inevitable that the fragmentation that we wrote about in the last chapter is to be a permanent feature of religion from now on? Or should one's attitude be to try, as it were, to keep both of these possibilities open to one's assent? Is it perhaps possible that all of these three options could be submerged by some new 'religious' approach of the kind that Luckmann has speculated about?[2]

Orthodox Catholics will have no difficulty about believing that their religion will indeed overcome all obstacles and remain essentially indefectible to the end. That is where the mystery of the Church, referred to in Chapter Two, comes in. At the same time, many Catholics are affected by the 'fragmentation syndrome' and would like to have it both ways, that is, feel themselves full members of the Catholic Church yet so pander to minority attitudes and issues — often at variance with official hierarchical teaching — as to marginalize themselves somewhat within the Church. And to the extent that such marginalization occurs, so also does the danger of an alienation from the Church along the lines already outlined, or at least a 'distancing' from the institutional Church.

It is within that kind of context that a drift can occur, away from one's handed down religious commitment to a new privatized — and ultimately secularized — religious transformation, almost without one realizing what is taking place. For the less educated and relatively uneducated (with whom today's mass society is brimming over — the football hooligans and mindless vandals being but frontline examples) genuine religious enthusiasm (to use a term very broadly employed by Ronald Knox[3]) can find a substitute in mass-entertainment and mass-rallies of all kinds, whether or not accompanied by drug addiction or alcohol abuse. There are writers on the sociology of religion who seriously contend that such enthusiasms can indeed be vicariously credited with catering for some of the functions once fulfilled by real religion[4].

On the part of the educated, the same process is seen as taking place when the cult of science, political parties or consumer goods, is made to fill the gap left in people's lives by the decay of their former religious commitment. Years ago, Jung used to think that such decay was almost the sole cause of neurosis. It still is a cause, without doubt, in some cases, but the opportunities for distraction are more numerous today, and man the breach, to a greater extent than before. Over the rest of this chapter, I propose to show how many modern intellectuals are trying to meet this situation.

Obviously, those of them who in any way favour the sort of immanentist theology that I wrote about earlier are easy prey for a secularist religious orientation. Already in 1961, the theologian Gabriel Vahanian noted that the conception of an immanentist world has involved the reduction of Christianity to the status of a 'civil religion'[5]. What he meant was that, especially in America, a secularist Protestant theology has steadily propelled American Protestant intellectuals in general towards an all-prevading secularism that has taken the place in every domain, including the sacred, of the outlook of their forefathers. How right he was emerges clearly when one finds the theologian Thomas Altizer arguing that the 'radical profane' may emerge as 'the sacred'. He goes so far as to say: 'In certain modern literary experiences of ecstasy in the midst of profanity there is a clue for developing a concept of an incarnation from within history' — a curious Christology indeed[6]. Signs on, we find the same Altizer elsewhere arguing that America should discover a meaning for itself that would be 'both redemptive and apocalyptic, redemptive in the sense of America's original promise of a liberation of a universal historical liberation of humanity, and apocalyptic in the sense of the Christian hope in a new and final victory of the Kingdom of God'[7]. All this while still maintaining that only the death of God 'can make possible the advent of a new humanity'[8].

In point of fact, an evolution of this nature is progressively taking place in America and, in a lesser but generically similar way, elsewhere. I am referring to the emergence of what has generally come to be called 'Civil Religion', following a 1967 essay by Robert Bellah, professor of sociology and comparative studies at the University of California, Berkeley. Its title was 'Civil Religion in America'[9]. Since then, Bellah has developed the concept in a book with the significant title of **Beyond Belief: Essays on Religion in a Post-Traditional World** (New York, 1970) and, with Phillip E. Hammond, professor of religious studies and sociology at the University of California, Santa Barbara, in **Varieties of Civil Religion** (San Francisco, 1980). A number of other scholars have, in one way or another, also taken up the idea by way a discussion of 'public philosophy' and 'public theology'[10].

While certain differences can be found between all of these writers, by and large they are talking about the emergence of a set of ideas, symbols and practices in the domain of social ethics and political morality that are independent of church teaching as such and that tend to arrogate to themselves an aura of religious solemnity. Indeed the thesis is that this owes its origin to an effort to get away from the Church-State conflict that has been such a marked feature everywhere in the past. At the same time, it is evident that secularization, with its attendant pluralism and privatization, is playing a major role in the thing. The basic contribution of secularization to the emergence of civil religion is its refusal to recognize religion as something that transcends all earthly powers yet, while placing great emphasis on the power of the State, subjects it to some ideology less specific than that of any Church. Pluralism is the more immediate fount, because through preventing any one religion from being a source of meaning for all, it spurs people to seek a generally acceptable meaning which, if found, they will naturally tend to cherish and exalt. Whether they know it or not, like it or not, people have an innate and undiscardable need for an overarching canopy which covers them all, a cement which causes them in some way to stick together, a universal corpus of significance onto which one and all may hang despite their many internal divisions and misunderstandings.

Taking his clue from the American scene, Hammond maintains that civil religion sprouts mainly from and finds its legitimation in educational and legal systems, each of which, in its own way, contributes to the elaboration of a framework of civilty, openness and tolerance, which elements, while they can and do go to constitute a distinct tradition wherever cultivated, avoid the feuds and prejudices of the past. In short, they can produce an ethos which, while allowing to all the maximum of freedom for the expression of their differences, joins them together at a 'neutral' level in an order that provides meaning.

THE LEGAL SYSTEM

The legal system performs a unique function in this, by which it becomes to some extent a replacement of the religious order and, in that sense, is an essential ingredient in the construction of a civil religion. It is easy to see how this can be so if we turn to what has happened in America. There, almost from the beginning, all religion (aside from some bouts of anti-Catholicism in certain States) was constitutionally free and to be tolerated. The elimination of the last vestiges of an Established Church in Massachusetts in 1833 could be said and has been said to have also eliminated Non-Conformity[11]. The State was a secular institution — religion being separated from the legislature, judiciary and executive. It was a matter for voluntary choice, a private affair. Despite this, the American people were genuinely religious, for which reason it has to be supposed that it was the diversity of their religious commitment (coming as they did from very different backgrounds) that imposed secularity upon them. Simultaneously, and again precisely because of their need to establish a national identity, the American people came to create 'the American way of life' in such a way that those values which might be regarded as most intrinsic to the respective denominations were soft-pedalled in the indiscriminate approval of religion of all kinds. Thus was the diminution of the effects of religious divergences achieved. It was a rather extraordinary performance really, because when one thinks hard on it one realises that it was a case of religious pluralism limiting itself through the fostering of less definite religious stances at any rate in the public forum. In practice (until recently when the American Catholic Bishops began staking out specific claims in the public-political and socio-economic spheres) it has meant that the American churches subordinated their distinctive religious values to the values of American society as a whole.

The legal system, and notably the courts, whether Supreme or of lesser level, has been central in providing the scaffolding for this. It is it which supplies the most fundamental element of a universal secular order. As Hammond puts it: 'The higher the level of religious pluralism in a society, the more will societal complexity depend upon, and thus be associated with, the presence of a universalistic legal system'[12]. The courts articulate, interpret and justify the law, giving reasons for their decisions. By that fact alone, they take on a kind of 'religious' character. When one adds to that a latent and indeed frequently overt assumption that the people under this legal umbrella are endowed with a manifest destiny, even a divine mission, a further 'religious' dimension enters in. To quote Hammond again: 'If in addition the agencies of this legal order use the language and imagery of purpose and destiny, if they not only resolve differences but also justify their resolutions, it is easy to see how something identifiable as civil religion could emerge.

There would exist already a cadre of "clergy", a set of "rituals", places for "worship", and a number of directives for "behaviour". Add to these a "theology" — an ideology of purpose and destiny or theodicy — and a civil religion may be close behind'[13]. It is worth noting that it was the Jesuit writer, Fr John Courtenay Murray, who in the 1950's first advanced the thesis that the American way was the only proper way for conducting politico-religious affairs. Significantly his book was entitled **We Hold These Truths**[14]. Even though the phrase was not current at that time, his critics saw his views as promoting 'civil religion'. It is possible that Talcott Parsons put the matter in its best perspective when he wrote: 'The contemporary Catholic, Protestant or Jew, may with variations within his own broader faith, even for Catholics, be a believer in the wider societal moral community . . . and . . . this common belongingness means sharing a religious orientation at the level of **civil religion**'. I forget in which of Parson's many writings this statement occurs. It might well be in his contribution to **The Culture of Unbelief** (University of California Press, 1971), or his article 'The Church in an Urban Environment' (cf. **Religion's Influence in Contemporary Society**, Columbus, 1972).

Parsons' analysis was right, but he did not follow it up. He spoke, as too many others also do, in blinkers. Alvin Gouldner, whom I have referred to earlier, put Parson's position well when he wrote: 'The Parsonian "sacred" thus no longer has an icon, a cult, or a God. It is an unexplained protoplasmic sentiment'. Once again, I cannot trace the exact location of this quotation, but I can praise Gouldner for his acuteness. Whether it be in Kant, Hegel, Husserl, Heidegger, and many besides, as Harrington also says, there is a compelling sociological argument that 'God cannot die', brought into the social sciences by men such as Alfred Schutz, Th. Luckmann and those others who ascribe to the thought of sociologists who are aware of the complexity of human life and insist in expressing it.

It is interesting to note that Bellah states categorically that from the point of view of republicanism, civil religion is a must. As an active political community, he says, a republic must have a purpose and a set of values. This is true. Every political community does so and the choice of values and their mentors is wide. But for historical reasons, allied to unbelief in France and, one might almost say, overbelief in America, the modern republican tradition has come to prize freedom — freedom from religious guidance included as paramount. In the end, the only worship that it espouses may be that of the republic itself as the highest good, with complementary rhetoric about cherishing all its citizens equally, but without adhesion to any special ecclesiastical relevance in the political domain. One hears that kind of thing whenever a claim is made to 'stand by the Republic' irrespective of Church utterances in politico-moral matters. Civil religion can be around the corner in such kind of republicanism.

In spite of its hopes, it need not be expected to solve the basic problem relating to the reconciliation of pluralistic interests. Again, the American experience is worth attending to. There, despite the development of a civil religion, as described, with all its overtures towards satisfying everybody by way of what is intended to be an official secularism, there is an ongoing battle concerning court decisions between minorities committed to their traditional religious values and the majority who adopted the civil religion of the American way of life. Questions such as denominational schooling, prayers in public institutions, abortion, divorce, homosexuality, etc. still constitute running sores which the ideology of civil religion cannot surmount, even with the help of the most vigorous efforts of its legal instrumentation.

TECHNOLOGICAL EDUCATIONISTS

It will be remembered that those who are most prominent in the sociological examination of the nature of civil religion also regard the educational system as its other most potent instrumental help. The thinking behind this has been lucidly expounded by Alvin Gouldner, to whom reference has already been made a number of times[15]. It is Gouldner's contention that the contemporary period has witnessed the appearance of a New Class, a class of intellectuals or intelligentsia deriving from its technological social integument. It derives too from the pluralism of modern European polity, which, unlike the Europe of former times, imposes no uniform set of basic norms but is rather a hotch-potch of fundamentally differentiated cultures, the result of which is often the migration of dissenting academics — **litterateurs**, scientists and theologians — from their original environments to others more congenial to their tastes. It is something which we can find borne out in the experience of many universities and Churches who have 'lost' quite a large number of their staff members, especially over the past thirty years. It has meant a criss-crossing of European intellectuals from one country to another, on a scale never witnessed since the Middle Ages. But there is a great difference between the current reasons for it and those of the medieval period. At that time it was caused by the homogeneity of European culture. Today it is caused by its diversity. Indeed it has been remarked that, apart from the political and economic cocoon of the EEC, with its multitudinous rules and regulations, mainly dealing with the technical coordination of affairs, about the only 'cultural' element in common among the member States is a certain 'European look', as to be seen in the cut of sartorial fashion, the **je ne sais quoi** appearance of architectural creations — the general image which the EEC presents to the world. Even that is presently being eroded by the importation of American facades, Japanese automobiles and by the wider extension of the Community. There is little in the way of a deep-rooted, substantial, philosophical or religious culture, the furthering of which was one of the principal aims of the original founders of the Community. Each of the countries which comprise it tends therefore to have dissidents who can change to other **ambiances**. Many have opted and continue to opt for going farther afield, notably to the 'anonymous market', of the USA.

To return more directly to Gouldner: it is his contention that the mobility of intellectuals, so characteristic of our times, coupled with their technical educational formation, goes to construct a New Class that is having an extensive influence on our civilization. He notes that an array of studies have shown that the education imparted by modern universities and institutes of higher technology tends to secularize students, along the lines that we have treated of earlier in this book. From it all you do get a New Class, a breed of intellectuals that is the product of secularism and pluralism. And, just as is the technological society that goes with them, they are to be found both in the capitalist and the socialist blocs. This New Class is quite unlike what Marx called the 'bourgeois class', whose radix was capital (deriving from property and exploitation), or what Djilas in his day also called the 'new class', whose radix was privilege. Gouldner's New Class rests on what he calls cultural capital, that is, the intellectual reserves of its members.

A NEW CLASS

The characteristics of this class are rather curious. In the first place, its members give allegiance to nobody but themselves. This is due partly to the fact that some of them come from the old 'moneyed' class but are culturally closer to their peers from the 'working' class (the product of modern free secondary education and third-level scholarships), as a result of which they sometimes conduce to a kind of 'civil war' within the 'upper' classes, while those of them who come from the working class are in their turn considerably separated from that class by reason of their possession of cultural capital. In brief, the New Class is not legitimated by any reference to social status. Its adhesiveness pertains entirely to itself, its genetic educational inheritance, its 'tribal' mores, in particular its linguistic code in virtue of which communication within it is sustained and justified not at all by the social status or authority of the speaker but by what he says and how he says it. Its central mode of influence is precisely communication — talking and writing.

It thrives on what Gouldner calls a 'culture of critical discourse'.

It is undeniable that he is very near the bone. Anybody who is familiar with the realms of higher technical education will recognize what he is after. There is such a thing as a peculiar 'speech community' going with those that staff these realms. It is oftentimes intriguing to the outsider, the 'layman' would be a better term. It is a jargon all its own. For example, instead of speaking about an authoritarian approach to questions, one will hear the technocrats speaking of 'Czarism'. Instead of speaking about a meeting to discuss problems, they will speak of an 'interface'. Instead of speaking about a point of crisis, they will speak of 'criticality'. Instead of speaking of the thinking out of a problem, they will speak of 'motoring' it. It is a jargon equalled only by that of some sports commentators who use phrases such as 'playing with conviction'. The technocrats have in fact virtually constructed an entire new vocabulary. This has its drawbacks as well as its advantages. While having the advantage of forging a bond among the technical intelligentsia themselves, it also makes for some cleavage between them and humanistic intellectuals. Indeed, as noted by Jurgen Habermas, there is an internal struggle within the New Class, between the new technocratic élite and the older humanistic élite[16], a struggle in which speech forms play their part. One can find aspects of this use of speech that is a feature of modernity outside the area of technology in the usual sense, in what should be entirely non-technological domains but which are affected by the emphases of the modern world. Scripture studies which use the methods of computer analysis are an instance. Even theology, as such, is not unaffected, as readers of modern theological literature, both Catholic and Protestant although more widely Protestant, know. It accompanies the type of approach to religion that Pierre Debray spoke of in the book (referred to in Chapter Three, note 14) entitled **The Technocrats of the Faith**.

A primary feature of the New Class is its proclivity towards dissent, an antipathy to all established tradition and authority. Gouldner actually says that while serving the society which pays for them, modern third level institutions also contribute to subverting it, by way of the generation of dissent through their culture of critical discourse. Habermas views the New Class as endangering not alone governmental authority but decision moulding by the populace at large. While himself espousing a Critical Theory of society, he is suspicious of that section of the New Class which is constituted by the technical bureaucrats. Whether or not one accepts Habermas's views on this, one can certainly understand why Gouldner regards the New Class in general as politically revolutionary and anti-establishment. The special reason for this radicalizing is an alienation on the part of intellectuals, an alienation fostered by a blockage in the way of their social ascent that is felt by many of their members. Hence their 'critical discourse', taking part in which itself, by its very nature, distances them from the conventional social hierarchy and is therefore, to a greater or lesser extent, a counter-force to that hierarchy, which is 'looked down' upon by the intellectuals. In truth, that is sometimes to be found as regards the Church hierarchy, vis-a-vis some theologians of today, even though, frequently enough, their ecclesiastical superiors may have been former professors of theology. Apparently, once one leaves the ranks of the New Class by way of 'upward' promotion or accession, one is presumed to have ceased being an intellectual and forfeited one's cultural capital. What Gouldner has to say in this connection is worth quoting and holds good in many spheres: 'The technical intelligentsia of the New Class is controlled by those incompetent to judge its performances and whose control, therefore, is experienced as irrational. The New Class intelligentsia, then, feel a certain contempt for their superiors; for they are not competent participants in the careful discourse concerning which technical decisions are made'[17]. This was certainly one of the reasons for the May Revolution of 1968 in France, with its call for formal 'participation' by students and other intellectuals in the direction of the affairs of society. It was a reason too for the campus revolts of 1969 in the U.S., as well as the opposition to the Vietnam War, which brought down the Presidency of Lyndon Johnson. In the case of Nixon, one could also see the hand of the New Class in the role played by the intellectuals of the media, who themselves are quite often not really the masterminds of a secular conspiracy so much as victims of the secularist vogue.

Thus there exists and flourishes a class, involved in education, which is a semi-autonomous group, with no allegiance to the class interests of students or their parents but devoted to speaking in the name of society as a whole, without any feeling of obligation towards preserving any particular interests or values other than its own, and in the case of values that means a 'free for all' or 'value free' stance. It is here that we are on the threshold of fathoming how this can conduce to civil religion. Ensuing confrontations are unavoidable, confrontations that are anomalous when (as I have mentioned in the case of theologians but which can happen in any sphere) the tensions are between rank and file members of the New Class and former members who have become incorporated into the officialdom that their erstwhile colleagues either never aspire to or find themselves blocked off from for other reasons. With or without becoming 'officials', in general members of the New Class do desire to 'have a say' in the fashioning of practical things (without any real practical responsibility). It is an age-old academic penchant but it is alive and well and active.

CIVIL RELIGION

The New Class advances civil religion insofar as it attempts to provide society with its own encompassing view of the universe. Not that all its members are atheists or agnostics, although quite a few are. But in one way or another all are pragmatic nihilists in that, whether they realise this or not, nothing is sacred to them. Their bedrock concern is the technical effectiveness of their work, the rationality and morality of which they and they alone will decide upon. When the operators of the legal system (the judges) make decisions with authority, they are decisions on the part of past members of the New Class. Politicians too can play a similar role. Such intellectuals expect a similar performance from all their peers, to the point, to use Gouldner's language, of requiring 'doctrinal conformity' and embodying aspects of 'ritualism and sectarianism'. There, once more, you have civil religion. None of these **aficionados** would be pleased to be labelled 'sectarian', but a broadening of mind rather than of that concept is all that is requried to see that they qualify for the appellation. It is puzzling why people like these who strive after secularization should, in the pursuit of their objective, come to sacralize the very methodology and accomplishments of secularization. Hammond in the book **Varieties of Civil Religion** opines that 'if a people who are so diverse that pursuit of their commonwealth would be precluded learn ways to engage in the pursuit, it is not surprising to find them honouring — even worshipping — "those ways"'. This is a rather stark statement of the situation, but the underlying train of thought is clear. Perhaps, after all, Comte was not far wrong when he proposed the rather startling idea in his time that the final stage in the evolution of Positivism would be a secular religion. If that is what civil religion is, he was nearer the mark than was realised.

THE MODERN HERESY

An American scholar, Martin E. Marty, has gone beyond analyzing the phenomenon of which we have been treating. He defends it as the only rational and workable future for religion. Right enough, he calls it 'the modern schism'[18] but goes on to explain that his choice of this term was designed to indicate that secularization does not mean the disappearance of religion so much as its 'relocation'. Really he should be speaking of 'heresy'.

Arguing that during the last century, there occurred a concatenation of events that were both more devastating to and more hopeful for Christianity than anything that happened during such periods as the Renaissance and the Enlightenment, he traces components in the 'modern schism' of secularization which, he maintains can be put to good use by religiously minded people. These components, he contends, are to be found in America, a country which unlike France and Italy and parts of Germany that either attacked or ignored religion, has — through the common sense of the members of its mainline Churches — transformed those Churches in a way that is a 'controlled' secularization. Whereas in places like Protestant Germany (through the work of Bruno Bauer and David Friedrich Strauss) religion became the worship of an incarnate God of mankind itself, and whereas in England it deteriorated into what H.G. Wells once called 'everydayishness' (its ministers becoming superfluous in men's scientific enquiries, many Bishops becoming near Deists, and minority Catholics conspiring with their environment to live decent and peacable lives — in sum all going their own way as 'unconscious secularists'), the United States took a different road. It did not attack, it did not ignore, but it came to terms with the modern age by replacing the older ecompassing religious culture by an inner, more private, one that still influences society to an important extent. Religious leaders came to monitor, inspire and sometimes legitimize aspects of secular culture (and were permitted to do so in a very open way — invocations preceding and blessings following legislative assemblies and public events). But Churchmen were not expected to offer systematic comment on the substance of legislation; that would be 'meddling in politics'. (I have already noted that the American Catholic Hierarchy at present seems to be challenging that.) People tacitly agreed to coexist, without crossing the cultural divides that make up the patchwork quilt of the American nation. And so there was little tension or militancy between religious 'ideologies'. Sacred symbols were easily switched to changing national purposes and the consensus of the Republic, enshrined in its legends and laws, became the touchstone of its public religion. To quote Marty: 'A lay religion, a radically altered religious construct, devised right under the noses of the clergy and with their unwitting help, was well on the way to formulation'[19].

All this, he says, happened during the course of the nineteenth century. The twentieth century has witnessed its apogee. Today's secularized American churchgoers are not at all secular, either in their own minds or as found in Europe: 'They have experienced a transformation of symbols, have found their own acceptable exegetes and mentors, have "made things come out right" somehow'.

Marty has followed up this 1969 book with another of 1981 in which he goes much further into the idea of the 'public Church', as found in America[20]. Once again he insists that, even though it is the fruit of modernity, that modernity 'merely dislocated and relocated the sacred', the durability of the sacred being rediscovered in the framework of secularization. He has no hesitation in acknowledging the role of 'tribalism' in the sense that just because modernity erodes the spiritual boundaries around people, imposing on them the privatist vogue of complete individualism of religious choice and practice, they always need to find an identity in common with others. Therefore, side by side with privatization, a certain totalism is beginning to prosper in religion, a system whereby people are learning to combine private religious commitment with civilty, a 'spiritual passion with a public sense' that overrides religious differences. Instead of Bellah's term 'civil religion' (derived originally from Rousseau), Marty prefers the term 'public religion'.

To quote him again. This type of religion, he says, "ministers to one part of life but not to another. Public life divorces itself from private faith. One should not mingle religion and politics or economics. The litany goes on: I cannot connect the faith I know on weekends with my job during the week . . . God is in a box marked sacred, and most activity is in a box marked secular . . . Problems result for all the traditional roles of the Church . . . To whom is the act of preaching to be directed, if the audience is made up of people each of whom has already established a trajectory of life, and who present themselves in a congregation only so long as the message conveniently reaches an individual and on that particular course? The audience turns out to be segmented, and is not really a congregation. The congregational style then changes and becomes a loosely connected set of specialities"[21].

At the moment there is a backlash against this in America, an effort at 'demodernizing'. Jerry Falwell and the 'moral majority' represent the Protestant wing of it. Even if they do go overboard at times in their enthusiasm, they scarcely merit being called 'subversives', as Daniel C. Maguire (a Catholic) has done in a vicious critique of what he calls 'the anti-Americanism of the Religious Right'[22]. And as Protestant leaders have begun to talk about issues ranging from the Vietnam War, civil rights, poverty, social justice, apartheid, so too Catholic leaders have begun to do the same, eschewing the 'civilized politeness' of a 'wholesome neutrality' for the 'wholeness' in life that the philosopher Paul Natorp perceives as absolutely essential to man. To the extent that this new development may succeed, Marty's optimism about the public side of his 'public Church' may be warranted, but never to the extent of whittling down dogmatic and moral loyalty to the institutional Church.

'THE NAKED PUBLIC SQUARE'

There is considerable evidence emanating from America right now that at least some of Marty's optimism is well founded. I am not referring to the proliferation of fundamentalist groups but rather to the kind of thing on the Protestant side that is embodied in the moral stances of President Reagan (as against the vapid liberalism of former President Carter) and on the Catholic side a whole range of thinking and writing (from Kirk Kilpatrick to Germain Grisez) as well as a swelling number of the ordinary faithful, and the growing assertiveness of the Hierarchy in public affairs.

What Richard J. Neuhaus (who has collaborated with Peter Berger in a number of projects) in his book **The Naked Public Square** called for, namely, a return of religion to the **areopagus** and the **forum**, is taking place and rather rapidly in America. Indeed the message of his book is that civil religion is outdated and that those who think otherwise are misreading the signs of the times[23].

The reasons for this decline in the 'ideology' that has been such a prominent feature of America for quite some time are many. For one thing the kind of theoretical consensus on which it chiefly rested has been badly shaken by the emergence of the 'New Right'. Its basic claim that there existed a core moral consensus, despite differences in religious belief, will not wash now. In any case, there exist many groups who would exclude religion even from the constricted public space which it has been accorded in the way of public oaths, prayers at legislative gatherings, and so forth. For, liberalism and all that withal, there has always been a current on the American scene that would not only bar religion from ever really 'belonging' in public space but would block it, insofar as possible from even impinging on it. There is also the fact that it has proved genuinely difficult to accomodate a variety of moral stances on the part of churches whose claims for the recognition of their socio-political positions are often enough irreconcilable. This difficulty is exacerbated by the fact that the democratic **ethos** entails that no party should be regarded as the custodian of moral rectitude in a way that might imply that others were immoral. And to crown it all, is an increasing awareness that State law — the main instrument of civil religion — simply cannot cover the diversity and mystery of human life.

By its very nature the ideology of civil religion emasculates itself and forces itself to be but a palliative with no forceful political thrust. Pro-Left liberals do not normally wish to disturb civilty provided the Right is reasonably 'contained', while their more aggressive Anti-Right brethren are generally cute enough to avoid confrontation on issues because such usually only strengthens the Right, which is a master of confrontational strategy. Hence it is that civil religion has regularly come to be seen as a 'fudging' of issues and, although it is certainly more than a code of politeness and courtesy and does wish not only to cultivate restraint on the part of all in the **civitas** but to elaborate a vision that they can share, it has not been able to live up to that since a substantial number of American citizens began to doubt whether everything their country stood for was good and in conformity with the larger purposes of God in world history. A sense of shared responsibility is required for the maintenance of the civil religion that was part and parcel of latter-day American liberal democracy. Alas, experience has shown that, as Neuhaus puts it 'it is a false consciousness to think that even the most intensive empathy can create a solidarity of identity and experience'[24].

To put all this in another way, we can say that, wish it in though they may have tried, the American people have not been able to prevent 'civilty' from becoming form without substance. To quote Neuhaus again: 'The bonds of public belonging have been dissolved. . . . At the heart of our communal discontent is that which . . . results from the hollowing out of meanings. . . . We exult in the gutting of them. This we call autonomy, liberation, freedom. We are liberated from duty, from honour, from country. It is the freedom of the naked public square'[25].

In that square there is no accepted authority that is higher than the **civitas** itself and loyalty to the **civitas** can be nurtured properly only if the **civitas** is not the object of highest loyalty. Certainly, patriotism alone cannot but lead to an overweening national pride, for which reason it needs to be ordered by a more encompassing 'piety'. Only traditional religion can provide this, because 'without a transcendent or religious point of reference, conflicts of values cannot be resolved; there can only be procedures for their temporary accomodation'[26]. By reason of the fact that this **lacuna** in civil religion has appeared consistently in recent decades, there has resulted what somebody has aptly called 'politics as civil war carried on by other means'.

And so, civil religion is being gradually put to one side — except for some trappings — and the State is stepping in and taking over. When, following a succession of court cases, religion is legally held to be a radically individualized and privatized matter, when it is held to be no longer a public reality of which public affairs should take account — such an 'evacuation' of the public square cannot but lead to its 'occupation' by something else. 'When recognizable religion is excluded, the vacuum will be filled by **ersatz** religion, by religion bootlegged into public space under other names. . .. Secular humanism, in this case, is simply the term unhappily chosen for **ersatz** religion. More than that, the notion of the secular state can become the prelude to totalitarianism. That is, once religion is reduced to nothing more than privatized conscience, the public square has only two actors in it — the state and the individual. Religion as a mediating structure — a community that generates and transmits moral values — is no longer available as a countervailing force to the ambitions of the state'[27].

It is because of considerations such as these that totalitarian States, whether those of Hitler and Stalin or others of similar ilk, concentrate their attack on religion not on that of the individual, which can be dismissed as superstition, but on the institutions that promulgate and sustain belief in a transcendent being by whom the State can be called to judgement. The situation is that both conceptually and historically there is no alternative to a **de facto** State religion once real religion is driven from the public square. Neuhaus notes musingly how literally denuded is Red Square, Moscow (I have experienced it) in contrast to the feature of public squares generally to be crowded. And he adds that for anybody to say that totalitarianism 'can't happen here' is to indulge in 'whistling in the dark'. It is well known that totalitarian democracy is quite possible[28].

Apart from the disturbing idea of State totalitarianism in the field of religion is the equally disturbing fact that any such State involvement can only reinforce moral relativism in what is left of democracy in those political societies that allow religion to be pushed out of the public square. For no such State, unlike the non-democratic totalitarian régimes, has a ready-made package of moral absolutes available and to be unchangeably upheld. In fact, its only absolute is an openness to the relativization of all values. It introduces a religion of relativity.

What to do to avoid this conundrum is something else. Some may be tempted to throw in the towel, saying that nobody knows the truth and, even if they did, it could not be respected in the cauldron of public life. Others may seek to avoid the issue by arguing that politico-moral questions are 'pre-political' or 'meta-political' and outside the domain of tractable politics. Others may strive for a system of compromise, on the grounds that after all the world is imperfect and democracy is a product not of a vision of perfection but of a knowledge of imperfection. Some may opt out by way of what they would regard as the honourable alternative of sectarian withdrawal (I use 'sectarian' in its original and proper sense). Still others may assume the mask of acceptance of the dilemma, on the grounds that their toleration of what they disagree with but do not combat in public is a toleration of necessity and not of principle. For these, democratic compromise is not at all a caving in to those for whom all truth is relative. They do not regard compromise as a defeat or as the striking of a deal, but the best that can be done 'under God'. Yes indeed. We have heard such sentiments often. The undeniable thing about them though is that they do have to bring God into the picture. That has inevitably consequences, which Neuhaus has stated cogently: 'The public framework of moral reference cannot sustain itself, it cannot stand on its own feet, so to speak. It needs to be attended to and articulated. This is the task not just of individuals but of institutions, most particularly the institutions of religion'[29].

1 Th. Luckmann, **Das problem der Religion in der Modernen Gesellschaft** (Freiburg im Breisgau), 1963; English translation: **The Invisible Religion** (New York, 1967).
2 Cf. also Kathleen Bliss, **The Future of Religion** (London, 1969), especialy Chapter VI, entitled 'Adherents'.
3 R.A. Knox, **Enthusiasm: A Chapter in the History of Religion** (Oxford, 1950).
4 See Bryan R. Wilson, **Religion in a Secular Society: A Sociological Comment** (London, 1966), pp. 15ff.

5 Cf. Gabriel Vahanian, **The Death of God** (New York, 1961), 49-51.
6 Th. Altizer, **Mircea Eliade and the Dialectic of the Sacred** (Philadelphia, 1963).
7 Altizer, 'Theology and Contemporary Sensibility', in W.A. Beardslee (ed.), **America and the Future of Theology** (Philadelphia, 1967).
8 Altizer, loc. cit.
9 In **Daedalus**, 1967.
10 Cf. Walter Lippmann, **The Good Society** (Boston, 1937); Martin E. Marty, **The Public Church**, (New York, 1981).
11 Cf. Bryan Wilson, **op. cit.**, Part II, 'Secularization in America'.
12 In R. Bellah and P. Hammond, **Varieties of Civil Religion** (San Francisco, 1980), p. 125.
13 Op. cit., p. 136.
14 John Courtney Murray, **We Hold These Truths: Catholic Reflections on the American Proposition** (New York, 1960).
15 See especially Alvin Gouldner, **The Future of Intellectuals and the Rise of the New Class** (New York, 1979).
16 J. Habermas, **Legitimationsprobleme im Spätkapitalismus** (Frankfurt am Main, 1973); English translation: London, 1976.
17 Gouldner, op. cit., p. 51.
18 Martin E. Marty, **The Modern Schism** (New York, 1969).
19 Op. cit., p. 124.
20 Martin E. Marty, **The Public Church** (New York, 1981).
21 Op.cit., p. 21.
22 Daniel C. Maguire, **The New Subversives** (New York, 1982).
23 Richard John Neuhaus, **The Naked Public Square** (Grand Rapids, 1984).
24 Op. cit., p. 67.
25 Op. cit., p. 75.
26 Op. cit., p. 110.
27 Op. cit., pp. 80 and 82.
28 Cf. Lord Percy of Newcastle, **The Heresy of Democracy**, (London, 1954) and J.L. Talmon, **The Origins of Totalitarian Democracy**, (London, 1952).
29 Op. cit., p. 221.

6

Reintegrating Religion and Life

I would see in analysis of the foregoing chapters a pressing need to highlight transcendence rather than immanence in Church theory (that is theology) and Church praxis (that is behaviour). We must, in other words, cultivate not only what Max Weber called 'inter-worldiness'[1], that is, a capacity to reflect on and relate to and act upon the world, but also what Christians have always espoused as 'other-worldiness', namely, a seeking after the things of Heaven.

By this, I mean fundamentally a searching for the sacred and bringing it more definitely into life in general. Molnar and Benoist, to whom Chapter 1 of this book is devoted, are in agreement about this but, as we know from that same chapter, differ profoundly in their understanding of how it should be accomplished. Benoist is a pagan, Molnar a Catholic.

For paganism, the sacred is to be found in nature, the substratum of the gods. It is therefore something immanent. For Christianity it is not so. Rather is nature itself a creature of the one transcendent God. The charge that Christianity has been the cause of desacralization by destroying the ancient cosmos forgets that Christianity introduced a new concept of the sacred, a sacred that is a mediator to the world of an extra-terrestrial transcendent, a God external to the universe. And the same Christian foundation of that concept is not myth either but the solid contents of the Scriptures. We have spoken enough already about those writers (whether for or against Christianity in principle) who would reduce Scripture to myth and then go on to demythologize it. That path is not only unnecessary but positively disastrous for Christianity.

Molnar puts his finger on it when he says that it is not the Christian Church but the vehicle of Christian civilization that has let things down by going in for the sort of thing to which I have just referred. What he means is that it is the society in which the Church exists that is the culprit, so to speak. Christianity, having desacralized nature (which simply means, having destroyed paganism as it was, in the Western world at least) went on to sacralize history, only to find, after centuries of effort that the world of history has been only all too ready to return to paganism and has been unfaithful to the Church of Christ.

'BACK' TO NATURE!

This year, 1986, has seen the publication in France of another fascinating book '(**Manifeste archaïque**)' by Laurent Dispot[2]. It is not necessary for our purposes here to go into detail as regards what he means by 'the archaic'. Suffice it to say that it does not necessarily coincide with the 'old'. Rather does it signify a way of thought that is not 'modern', and which, in fact, contradicts many modern presuppositions and acceptances. Much of what it has to say deals with the modern return to nature, which Molnar would regard as a form of paganism. We must be content with a few examples.

'Liberalism' is one, regarded as the most natural philosophy possible because it reflects the 'law of the jungle'. The truth is that nothing could be more contrary to the law of the jungle than liberalism, because the law of the jungle is a law of the preservation of an equilibrium. The 'cult of the body' (whether body building, nudism and the rest) is another example. Nudism is regarded as natural, a return to nature (the **Freikorperkultur** as some Germans call it), whereas the truth is that nothing could be more artificial because it is one of the most basic human tendencies to clothe oneself, for climatic reasons if for none other. The cult of suntan (**Bronzification** as some French call it) is an example in the same vein. The truth is that a practice that, if overdone, can lead to skin cancer can scarcely be natural. Yet another example is the contemporary craze about youth and youthfulness (le jeunisme) which even the old go in for. The truth is that it is natural to get old and that much of youth culture is created by the marketing of a consumer society. One could go on and on with such examples of the false 'naturalism' of today. Ecologism even falls into the trap, not the balanced interest in ecology which produces positive results, but an ecologism that is really a nihilism (animal liberation enthusiasts being prepared at times to kill people so as to preserve animals or plants!). The truth is that it is not natural for man to quit developing the earth. On the contrary that is his destiny and his privilege, as cooperator with the Creator, doing it with consideration and care. Pacifism is also regarded as the most natural thing of all. Sure, everybody wants peace, but the truth is that human nature is such that one has to keep the peace all too often by preparing for war. It is surely ironical to find civil rights and pacifist promoters becoming militants and even terrorists in the name of their humanist ideals. Abortion too is said to be natural because it is right for a mother to 'assist' nature, already 'overpopulated', by lessening the number of people in the world. The truth is that if nature is the greatest abortionist, it should be logical to kill off all the handicapped, all those races which the dominant ones despise — no longer to talk of genocide. Against that perspective, it should be logical too to kill off baby seals, indeed for their mothers to do so! Homosexuality is also defended by some as natural. No comment.

All kinds of other practices come to mind that are accepted as natural — the use of tobacco, of alcohol, even the motor car. The truth again is that these things have become 'naturalized' rather than that they are natural in themselves. It is certain that in some ways they are part of man's proper development of his world, but in other ways they can prove excessive and mistaken. Viewers of the Ewings, the Colbys and the Carringtons will surely recognize what I mean. Perhaps the most foolish form of 'naturalization' is that which has been progressively employed by some politicians who presume to think that they can run a country by relying on statistics and opinion polls as portrayers of what is 'naturally expected' or the 'done thing'. The truth is that such devices are the negation of political philosophy and rational political thought and have proved themselves to be so so often now that it is hard to find them still acted on. In fact, they are sometimes used in such a way as to constitute a quite improper pressure in democracies. Let us finish with one further example of the contemporary 'return to nature' — the cult of astrology. The newspapers and magazines are full of the thing, telling us how to be guided by nature in the context of 'our stars'. There is much more to it. In France, practically the entire series J'ai Lu is devoted to 'natural mysteries', also many publications from the publishing house of Robert Laffont and even some from Editions du Seuil. The truth is that all such initiatives remove one from nature rather than the opposite.

The fact of the matter is that the very concept of 'nature' has become deformed since the eighteenth century. In virtue of an extrapolation of the idea of man as a liberated private individual, nature has become the reflection of man's artificial constructions and purely personal pursuits. It has become something that is seen as resting on individual liberty rather than on a universal order which furnishes it with a rational guarantee, an order which, as St Thomas Aquinas explained, also heals, perfects and raises up a wounded human nature without destroying it. Such nature is as respectful of its creator as it is a source, indeed the only source, of a true humanism. It transcends itself and enables man to do likewise by its relationship to God. In his address at Cervia on 11 May 1986, Pope John Paul II drew attention to the sacred character of nature, as found in the sea and the fields (**L'Osservatore Romano**, English edition, 16 June 1986), with a reminder of the fundamental values of human and Christian spirituality, orientated towards God.

'DOWN' TO TRANSCENDENCE!

So great is the downward pull of this world that, at the present time, there are quite a number of thinkers (philosophers, sociologists, even theologians) who are prepared to maintain that it is possible to give full commitment to a secularized society and simultaneously to transcend it without any form of commitment to traditional Christianity, if indeed to belief in God. They are well aware of the need to transcend our world, to get away from being cabined and confined by technology, and to find that compulsive power over our minds that draws us to realms beyond ordinary experience. Even Sir Julian Huxley, the doyen of scientific humanists, saw that[3]. Peter Berger manages to combine his excursions into the sociology of knowledge, which I so much admire, with a well-intentioned but not yet quite successful effort towards transcendence, in that it is simply not possible to construct the aura and awe of transcendence on the bare foundations of philosophical anthropology[4]. Charles Hartshorne and the defenders of Process Theology — an outlook not unlike that of de Chardin — see in man's capacity for even greater growth an entrée into the transcendent, a being set free for the world by being set free from idolising it, yet still admitting only a faith that calls for a divinization of the world: man is on his earth and God is in his heaven[5].

All of these tentatives are aimed at some kind of sanctification of secular life, bringing the sacred and the profane more and more together[6]. They could be said to have reached their zenith in Alistair Kee's book **The Way of Transcendence**: **Christian Faith without Belief in God**[7]. Kee too is aware of the contemporary craving for transcendence, made evident by the enrolment of many 'good time' kids in secular caring organizations, militant movements for rights and even revolution, the non-violent activism of the New Left against the materialism of the affluent society, the popularity of eastern religions, such as Hare Krishna and Zen Buddhism, the growing appeal as well for many of the Western mystical traditions, and, of course, the widespread practice of trancendental meditation. Of a different and worrying nature is the current craze for superstition, spirit phenomena, astrology, exorcism . . . The hippies and the flower children were similar 'escapists', although now somewhat passé. Kee's solution has no great merit. For him, instead of talking about God or the supernatural, we should concentrate rather on what he calls the 'infinite' — that which limits man's achievement yet is also a never-failing source of power to men in the pursuit of achievement. It is a very contrived effort to seek transcendence yet deny God.

I am sure it will be realised that it is not for me here to try to outline the ways and means whereby a true concept of transcendence can be reintroduced into those areas in which it has been blurred. In his 1974 book, **The Recovery of the Sacred**[8], American Catholic, James Hitchcock, has provided us with a long list of what is needed. It ranges from the rehabilitating of as many religious symbols as possible that can mediate the presence of God, the restoring, wherever and to what extent is necessary, of an aura of mystery to the liturgy, the cultivating (without being open to the accusation of obscurantism) of all orthodox forms of popular devotion, including habits of prayer that are aided by means such as the rosary.

Hitchcock remarks shrewdly that the rekindling of a vivid faith at present requires a recovery of a sense of the importance of what Pascal called 'custom' in religion (I nearly said — 'old, forgotton, far-off things, and battles long ago'). In point of fact, it is intriguing to look back on the way that Chateaubriand in his **The Genius of Christianity**[9] was aware of this and emphasised it as a main source of the Christian thing. The fourth part of his monumental work comprises six books, devoted to ceremonies, feasts, missions, bells, church ornaments, hymns, prayers, rogation days, and much besides in like vein — and he dedicated it all to Napoleon Bonaparte!

Napoleon was a secularist, although the memoirs of his Irish doctor in St Helena would seem to indicate that he had a respect for real transcendence. Contemporary sociology too, **by its own**

admission, agrees that transcendence is essential to man and that it is only to be found outside the confines of sociology. It is up to all of us to do our best — for our own sakes and in the service of the Church — to find that transcendence in a humble following of Jesus Christ.

FAITH AND SOCIAL CHANGE

As a psychological help to that, we should realize that, even the most far-reaching human societal changes do not — and cannot — infringe the supernatural indefectibility of the Church of Christ.

It may indeed be a presumption on my part, but I refer in that connection to the results of a sociological survey which was conducted in my Diocese only a couple of years ago. It is **The West Limerick Study**, done under the auspices of the Social Science branch of the National Institute for Higher Education, Limerick[10].

That survey shows that the past two or three decades have seen very extensive changes take place in West Limerick. Some of these are demographic and occupational, namely, an increase in the population of the towns as against the villages and countryside, together with a growth in the numbers engaged in industry as against a contraction among those in agriculture.

This is something that Ireland as a whole has experienced, to a greater or lesser degree, during the same period. With it, in West Limerick as elsewhere, has gone a good deal of social and cultural change — in the amenities and living standards of the people, their pattern of mobility, their traditional attitudes and expectations.

Side by side with this, the study found that the various elements that go to constitute culture have not changed in the same way or to the same degree. It says that 'one of the most important findings of the study illustrates that change is neither all inclusive nor uniform in its effects. The selective nature of change is manifested by the fact that some people's lives are relatively untouched by the industrialisation process which is

119

proceeding apace in the area. Furthermore, traditional behaviour patterns and values coexist in many cases with modern, urbanised lifestyles and values, illustrating that traditional and modern are not necessarily imcompatible'.

As somebody who is committed to the retention of both our traditional Christian culture and our traditional Irish culture, as well as appreciative of the necessity and importance of a sound modernisation, I believe that one of the most significant contributions of that survey is a deeper understanding of how change and continuity can be reconciled.

The study of cultural change in advanced or relatively advanced societies is a fairly recent development in social anthropology. Until the 1950's or so, it was conducted almost exclusively in the context of primitive or at least peasant societies. When Arnsberg and Kimball did their study of West Clare in the 1930's[11], they did so against that background.

Since then, social and cultural analysis has turned progressively to an examination of more complex societies. West Limerick today cannot be said to fall into the category of a peasant society. Rather is it the product of a progressive evolution from pre-industrial agricultural society towards a full scale industrial urban civilization. It is somewhere in between the two.

Because of its implications for the rest of the Mid-West Region as well as for the country as a whole, I would like to outline here what I believe to be responsible for West Limerick managing — to date at least — to combine these diverse elements.

The basic question is: What causes cultural change? What are the social forces that are responsible for it and, equally, what is it that restrains it? It is accepted by the generality of sociologists that these causes are many. The Marxist contention that economic factors are the exclusive clue to it all is not upheld by the majority of scholars outside the classical Marxist ideological camp. Social causation is seen to be the product of many and diverse contributions.

In some cases social change is attributable to the decision

and efforts of outstanding individuals or groups. In other cases it can be due to structural modifications in society caused by, say, the immigration of large numbers of strangers. In still other cases it can be brought about by external influences through direct contact with other societies. And quite often, of course, social change is caused by the convergence of all of these factors, which, itself, can be fortuitous. Finally, an important cause of social change is the presence of a common purpose among the members of the community involved. By that I mean that if the majority of the community regard the change as on the whole desirable, a kind of unconscious process of willing it into being takes place. This particular cause of social change is extremely relevant in highly integrated small communities. All of these causes have played a role in the social change that has taken place in West Limerick and they have implications for much of the rest of the region, which, apart from the urban agglomeration of Limerick-Shannon, is basically similar in character.

The West Limerick Study underlines the fact that people choose their own pace (and space) in adapting to change. Such a view, it says, was articulated by some of its respondents when describing their attitudes to developements in the area. 'One of the most highly endorsed views was that change was acceptable only if it did not disrupt or destroy existing values and lifestyles in the area'.

In this connection, it is interesting to note that Lucy Mair, Professor of Applied Anthropology at the London School of Economics, in an 1964 paper entitled 'How Small-scale Societies Change', maintained that the real puzzle is not what causes social change but what makes conservatism tick[12]. For without the brake which conservatism imposes, change would be a runaway feature of society.

This is because social change inevitably means the introduction of new opportunities, new alternatives in life, and people are naturally attracted by that. Small-scale society, in particular, is profoundly affected by the possibilities of new opportunities, new choices, precisely because it is limited by its restricted scale and lesser technical infrastructure.

In any given society at any given time, and especially in small-scale society, people in general will tend to seize on the new opportunities that are offered to them by the creation of new situations. At the same time, some people — and even the people in general in some respects — can tend to cling to the manner of life in which they grew up. There can in fact be occasions when this engenders in them a crisis of conscience, as it were, that is, when the new roles which social change confers on them are incompatible with, or seem to be imcompatible with, obligations that they have for long accepted.

There is evidence in **The West Limerick Study** that this dilemma has surfaced to some extent in the area. Precisely because the expectations of the people in a largely agrarian and village environment are predominantly those of traditional rural life, some resistance to change is quite normal. It is easier to choose new roles where one is not surrounded by old expectations. This is underscored very clearly by the study when it says that 'people showed a certain level of nostalgia at the passing of the "old ways", although they did seem to be reconciled to the fact that development necessarily transforms some areas of their lives'.

FAMILY AND COMMUNITY

The study shows too that, in spite of the many changes that have taken place since the fifties, the nuclear family still remains a powerful social force. In this connection, undoubtedly one of the most influential segments within the family network are parents of the more advanced age group and grandparents. Not too many years ago, all over the world, it was these, almost exclusively, who engineered the destiny of society. In a book published in 1959, Margaret Mead described this type of thing as 'post figurative' culture, that is, a culture in which the model for the behaviour of the young is provided by the elders and in which there has been no great break in the acceptance of the ways of their ancestors. Not surprisingly, the title of the book was **Continuities in Cultural Evolution**[13].

Later, around 1969, she produced another book, entitled **Culture and Commitment: A Study of the Generation Gap**[14], in which she recognized that today society everywhere tends to be more a 'cofigurative' one, that is, one in which the prevailing model for the members is the behaviour of their contemporaries. 'In its simplest form', she says, 'a cofigurative society is one in which there are no grandparents present'.

Margaret Mead saw this as the better thing. It means less resistance to social change, which is implicitly accepted as meaning progress. I quote from her again: 'The transition to a new way of life, in which new skills and modes of behaviour must be acquired, appears to be much easier when there are no grandparents present who remember the past, shape the experience of the growing child and reinforce, inarticulately, all the unverbalised values of the old culture. The absence of grandparents . . . means the absence of a closed, narrow . . . community'.

It appears to me that **The West Limerick Study** does not permit one to classify the area under discussion as either a postfigurative or a cofigurative society. It is a mixture of both. I am in a position to know the extent to which grandparents are present and exert a quiet but effective influence at religious ceremonies, particularly Confirmations. I am equally aware of the tendency today for young people to disregard the attitudes of their elders. As Margaret Mead has put it, until very recently the elders could say: 'You know, I have been young and you have never been old'. But today's young people can reply: 'You never have been young in the world I am young in, and you never can be'.

That, of course, is true and it is the reason why the generation gap is fraught with meaning and consequences. In the West Limerick scene, it means that right now there exists what sociologists know as a cultural lag, in other words, an unequal rate of progression in the various aspects of culture. When its constituent parts do not change at the same rate, a rapid change in one part is not accompanied by parallel corresponding adjustments in other parts. It is this that creates the condition of lag. It is well to note, however, that the term 'cultural lag' is not necessarily a pejorative one. It all depends on the kind of change that is taking place and whether total adjustments to it are to be welcomed.

Here we enter the realm of value judgements. That this is entirely right and proper to our discourse is attested to by prominent exponents of the cultural lag concept who agree that whether an alleged lag is to be deplored or admired depends upon the value frame within which is is viewed. Peter Berger is quite definite that there is no reason whatsoever why all philosophical, moral, familial, educational and religious ways of thinking and acting should slavishly change in the wake of the technological change that is an inevitable part of modernization. If this be so, there is a place in society for those 'godfathers' who are 'grandfathers'! Grandmothers likewise. The past has got to acknowledge their role and the future should not despise it. There is a lot of truth in the French saying: **Tout est relatif**.

It is against this backdrop that we can begin to understand the reason why cultural change in West Limerick has not followed industrialisation in the way that some might have expected. It is also important to note that, as Margaret Mead pointed out in still another book, **Cultural Patterns and Technical Change**, published as long ago as 1955[15], the extent to which socio-cultural change affects the family depends, as she put it, on 'what has been there to begin with'.

In actual fact this is true of society as a whole and not just the family. It was perhaps the greatest contribution to social survey work of the (first) **Limerick Rural Survey** (1964) — although this has not been noticed by everybody who might have been expected to do so — that it highlighted the fact that cultural change does not take place in a vacuum but in the spatio-temporal dimensions that are associated with human geography and social history. I have dealt with this at some length in my book **New Dimensions in Regional Planning**, published in 1966[16]. And I am appreciative of the fact that **The West Limerick Study** has indeed made considerable use of historical data in its research. I mention this especially in view of the fact that this study says, towards its conclusion, that its findings suggest the need to examine the pace and direction of social change in more detail, and to investigate especially how modern and traditional coexist. I could not agree more.

Continuing study is needed on many facets of the impact of industrialisation in all areas. For one thing, what precisely is a person of a particular area and how can we be sure that random samples cover him or her as persons? This is a difficult problem, of the kind, for example, which would have faced sociologists, if there were any in those days, following the Norman conquest or the colonization of America. Another problem is the difference between a situation where a giant industrial plant is being constructed by a huge work force that is transitory as well as indigenous, and that in which industries are fully established and have permanent operatives. The extent to which human geography as well as social, economic and political history can throw light on the possibilities and ramifications of modernization is something that deserves closer attention. So too does the impact of power structures, whether local, regional, national or international. It would be a mistake, though, to regard the process of modernization simply as a manifestation of the spread of the capitalist system and all that it entails. Many areas of the Second as well as the Third World are presently undergoing similar change.

WORSHIP IN HISTORY

As far as Christianity is concerned, we ought to be under no doubt but that religion should be integrated with life, that the Church should be brought to where the people congregate in the pursuit of everyday affairs. Why should the market-place be cut off from them, as so many of our church buildings have unfortunately become?

In the days of early Christianity, things were very different. It is historically the case that villages over much of Western Europe, with their weekly markets, sprang up around the villas of Roman times as centres where the peasants from the surrounding countryside brought their produce for sale. A church was usually the centerpiece of these market-places.

As time went on, many of these settlements expanded into towns, some with a resident bishop and a cathedral, in the shadow of whose walls merchants of all kinds traded their wares. One account which I have come across says that, once started, if conditions were favourable, these towns grew like snowballs. Butchers, bakers, candlemakers, smiths, carpenters, tailors and so on all added in their services and created new consumer demands. Before long, the town was given a wall for defence and became what was known as a 'burg' or fortified place, the term from which the present word 'borough' takes its origin.

From time to time during the year, fairs were held around these cathedral precincts, some of them known throughout the length and breadth of Europe and named, as befitted events that were closely associated with religious surroundings, after the then popular saints. It is consoling to know that even siants can rise and decline in popularity! Thus it was that in Champagne the famous fair of St Jean was held at Troyes in July and August, that of St Ayoul (whom we in Ireland don't know about at all) was held in Provins in September-October, and that of St Remy, again at Troyes, in November and December. Likewise, in England you had the great fairs of St Ives and St Giles, saints who have had little impact in this country[17].

Many of these fairs originated as religious festivals. The fair at St Denis near Paris grew up about an open space between Montmartre and the city, where once a year in June a relic of the True Cross which had been acquired by the Cathedral of Notre Dame was shown to the people and traders were quickly attracted by the large numbers of pilgrims. There is an old artistic representation still existing which shows the Bishop of

Paris blessing the people on the occasion, with booths and standings of the merchants all around.

Against this backdrop of religion intermingled with their work, it was only to be expected that many trades and businesses were themselves called after saints. We find St Bartholomew as the patron of tanners, St John of candlemakers, St Crispin of shoemakers, St Mary Magdalen of perfumers, St Barbe of brushmakers, St Cloud of nailmakers, St Clare of mirrormakers, and so forth[18].

Before long too, during the high Middle Ages, we also find companies of these and other avocations binding themselves together each into associations or guilds, a great number of whose functions were religious, particularly of a charitable nature. They provided help for their ill and destitute members, contributions towards their hospital and funeral expenses, sometimes even making baptismal gifts when children were born to them. And, needless to say, they were generous in the extreme in the building of churches in their towns.

In the construction and furnishing of the catedrals individual wealthy burghers and the corporate guilds joined to make worthy contributions, often competing with each other in endowing such pieces as stained glass windows commemorating biblical anecdotes and stories from the lives of saints. In the case of Chartres, for instance, forty-two windows were donated by the town's guilds, who perpetuated their identities by means of panels illustrating their crafts.

THE SECULAR SOCIETY

It is indeed a set-back for religion that from early modern times on, Christendom has witnessed a progressive separation of religious and secular life, to such an extent that today people speak freely — too freely in fact — of the secular society as something to be welcomed and even furthered on every possible front.

There have been, it is true, some exceptions to this blind secularizing tendency. It is to the credit of the venerable and respected religious orders, particularly the Dominicans, the Franciscans, the Augustinians, the Jesuits and the Redemptorists, that they have always striven and by and large successfully, to stem this unfortunate trend. In city after city all over the Catholic world, they have laboured long and hard, through bad times as well as good, to provide churches right in the centre of commercial life. We owe them an immense debt.

But such efforts are no longer enough. Today city life is rapidly changing. The supermarket and suburban shopping centre are new features on the urban skyline. And it would appear that they have come to stay, certainly during the foreseeable future. They have become the nuclei of mini-towns, often stocked with products that are hard to come by in the older centres.

Actually, we should not be too hasty in denouncing all secularism. Insofar as it means that worldly concerns and values are given their due place and worth, it is entirely in accordance with what God, the Creator, intends. And, like humanism, true humanism, so also true secularism can have its rightful role and worth.

In this connection, may I draw attention to the way in which atheistic and even anti-religious ideologies have usurped the use of and arrogated to themselves such titles as 'rationalism', 'liberalism', 'socialism' and 'communism' — leaving the impression that anyone who is opposed to these is irrational, illiberal, asocial and non-communal, when in fact what one is rejecting is the irreligious overtones of these 'isms' as they have developed historically. It is the same with the use of the term 'secularism'.

The trouble is that all too often today we find ourselves confronted with a secularism that would elbow religion altogether out of public social life (whether political, legal, economic, educational and the like). We know only too well the trend towards excluding religious convictions from being reflected by law, whether statutory or constitutional. We know too the way in which politicians are pressurised to forget about religion in their catering for the common good, on the grounds that anything else would be sectarian. We know the extent to which religion is forgotten in those educational institutions which, when appointing staff, will look at a wide gamut of the candidate's qualifications, from professional achievements to hobbies, yet avoid all question of his or her religion. And we know how modern art has, by and large, abandoned religious inspiration.

It would be laughable, if it were not such a tragic distortion of reality, to find any recognition of religion on the part of secular concerns being labelled sectarian while many secular agencies indulge in their own kind of preaching. At the same time, some literary and artistic ventures whose thrust is veiledly antagonistic towards religion, or at least in some areas the religion of the majority of the people, can be supported out of public funds.

It is sad too that the media, at least at the national level, so frequently canvass points of view that are anything but impartial in matters connected with the Catholic Church. While there is indeed some excellent reporting of religious interest, it would be better, to say the least, if there were fewer biassed contributions in this domain.

Secularism can be a very insidious thing that sometimes eats even into the manners and customs of the Church itself. I am thinking of the way in which some Catholics manage to persuade themselves that they are faithful to their Church even though they reject some points of its teaching. I am thinking too of the way in which clerical and religious dress is sometimes put aside in circumstances in which it need not and should not be. For the very wearing of this 'uniform of Christ', if one may term it that, can itself be a significant witness to the following of Christ, mute yet quite effective.

The big danger about failing to give evidence of our religious persuasions in the domains of public life is that this is but a short step from extrapolating religion from all life, whether private or public. And this is exactly what has occurred where secularism has been allowed to evolve without check.

URBAN POSSIBILITIES

It is gratifying to learn that there is some optimistic thinking at present that sees possibilities in contemporary affluent and technologically dominated urbanism for the creation of an environment that would reduce privatization and reintroduce more community living of a kind that could help to humanize our society.

We noted in an earlier chapter the effects on people of the massive technological and bureaucratic culture that is a feature of our time. We noted too how this has contributed to a diminution in real social interaction. Whereas in the older, nineteenth century type cities, inadequate material resources compelled their dwellers to live in or near what we now call the inner city, simply because they did not have the money to move out to suburbs even if they would have preferred it, present-day city folk of even modest wealth can do so and are doing so as fast as they can in search of a coherent community life of the kind for which, as we know from Aristotle, man as a social animal craves.

We saw too that this life is by no means always or even generally found in the suburban residential areas which affluence today enables many people to choose for themselves and which urban planning provides for countless others. The failure of this has been due to the fact that these new areas seldom produce a true community solidarity based on people's need for each other, while conserving their equal need to preserve their personal and family identities.

This is because these environments all too often conglomerate their residents in groups rather than in real communities. It was the famous German sociologist Ferdinand Tönnies who, at the beginning of this century, made a distinction between 'group life' and 'community life', the former providing ties between people through common class interests that were in themselves emotionally neutral, the latter a life which enabled them to feel emotional ties with each other as full human beings. In the majority of today's suburbs, community is to be found mostly to the extent that those who live in them only feel that they are with their peers, people like themselves. While this at least gives them the consolation, if that is the right word, of having a 'sameness' around them, it has also deprived them of the confrontations and explorations of more multiple social contact points. In other words, the very affluence that has made the contemporary search for community open to so many, has frequently actually led to an isolation in community contacts, all the more so in that it has lessened if not eliminated the need for sharing, except in times of crisis, such as flooding or some other unusual occasions. Each family normally possesses all that it wants — domestic appliances, transport, water supply, heat. . ., at any rate in the wealthy suburbs. The American sociologist Richard Sennett has named this type of environment a 'destructive Gemeinschaft', adapting Tönnies' terminology to cover a community that for the greater part is only a group[19].

It is the family that suffers most in this situation. It is true that it provides the family with the kind of trust in stability that is all-important to its base, a belief that it is not subject to betrayal in such surroundings. The cost, depending on circumstances, is a certain turning in on itself. There is great cost too to the city as a whole. 'The family has appropriated the social functions and contacts that men once sought in the broader area of the city. This appropriation by the family of social "spaces" once felt inappropriate for the home has encouraged something perverse in the urban communal relations men have left, and in the family itself'[20]. As regards the family, psychologists tell us that this can result sometimes in the onset of neurosis of one kind or another and as regards the deserted inner city in an increase in violence and crime.

But Sennett also contends that things need not necessarily be like that. The clue, he is persuaded, could lie in the encouraging of new multiple points of contact, contact points that have died out in the city. What is wanting, he says, is the bringing back not of the old-time city, which would be impossible anyhow, but a city planning which, while allowing for an interpenetration of its various groups would also preserve the stability of the home. He has in mind a vigour of city living that would reduce the pressures on families whose inward-turned intensity of life together has limited the diversity of their experience. For a change to occur, the social space of cities has to be approached in a new way, making for opportunities for complex experience.

To this end the material wealth of today's urban societies — though limited in some places more than others — could be used as an agent of freedom. Naturally, planning is central to it all. Instead of Baron Haussmann's Paris, elegant though his boulevards may be, and instead of the gridiron pattern of New York and elsewhere, the higgledy-piggledy layout of some cities and large towns, with their narrow, winding streets, their nooks and passages and covered ways, is what creates the conditions for intimacy and true community at the hands of human geography.

With it would come a whole range of small shops, flats for young people, inexpensive family restaurants and the entire paraphanalia of a vibrant community life. The family would then have a more realitic and meaningful function as an intensive shelter for its members but as an integral part of community rather than of group living. It is all very idealistic, without doubt, but it is looking to the long-term future.

And if community is one of the features which, theologians assure us, is a crucial aspect of Christianity, then religion too would benefit from the ensuing curbing of privatization and its drawbacks. In such a context (far though it may be from being brought about) there is no reason to fear and condemn urbanism. In the past civilization and urbanism have gone hand in hand. They can also do so in the future. From that angle it would be unwarranted to decry secularism.

RELIGION AND CULTURE

Untrammelled secularism is a disaster both for private and public life. For private life it means the elimination of the healing bond between God and man, the self-destruction of man's salvific hope. For public life it means the elimination of the most important element in the development of culture, leaving human society adrift.

It was the great English Catholic historian of the pre-war and post-war period, Christopher Dawson, who perceptively saw religion as central to all culture. Whether in primitive times, the early Christian ages, the Medieval period, or later, Dawson saw man's development — in politics, law, literature, art or economics — as associated with religious belief and practice.

This is not the place in which to go into the considerations which influenced Dawson. Suffice it to say that he made more than a passable case for the claim that it is religion that was mainly responsible for the Western world's cultural legacy which the past has handed down to us.

During the Medieval period especially, it was Christian belief that was dominant in the fashioning of culture. It was the inspiration behind the warp and woof of the Medieval world, which reflected the faith in every aspect of its social life. But Dawson went beyond historical exposition. He divined rightly, and said so, that 'the only true criterion of a Christian culture is the degree in which the social way of life is based on the Christian faith. However barbarous a society may be, . . . if its members possess a genuine Christian faith, they will possess a Christian culture'.

In other words, the religious life of any people inevitably overspills into the organisation and pigmentation of the life of the society in which it is lived.

Marx himself was so aware of this that he argued that 'man emancipates himself by eliminating religion from public life and making it a private matter'. And yet, at the same time (as Lucien Goldmann has noted in his **Le Dieu Caché**, (Paris, 1955), even Marx could not get away from a realization of the absolute essentiality of the transcendent to man, his whole work being infused with the vision that the proletariat can, through struggle, create a transcendental of this world, called Socialism. The French Marxist, Roger Garaudy, understood this Socialist functional equivalent of religion. He wrote: 'Transcendence can mean belief in a world beyond, in the supernatural, with the irrationality, the miracles, the mystery and finally the deception that these notions carry with them'. Still, he went on: 'The claim to transcendence is the actual human experience that man, though belonging to nature, is different from things and animals and that man, forever able to progress, is never complete'. One could call this 'process theology' with a difference. That it acknowledges the need for the transcendent is certain.

It is a measure of the decline of Christian faith in our time that our social fabric has become so denuded of Christian influence. And it is with shame that we have to admit that, when it comes to upholding religious values in the context of law, politics, economics and the rest, the Moslem world is ahead of us, at least according to its own religious lights.

An English expert on that world — a non-Catholic as far as I am aware — has this to say in a book first published in 1979: 'Islam claims authority over everything the Muslim does, including his political and economic activities. For the devout Muslim a reference to a "secular Muslim country" is meaningless, a contradiction in terms; according to the Koran, a Muslim country is Islamic and to apply the adjective "secular" to it is pointless and even insulting. It is difficult for the West, where religion plays such a small part, or no part at all, in the lives of the vast majority, to understand the extent to which Islam is a whole way of life, reinforced daily by frequent communal observance'[21].

I do not say that the Moslem approach is to be copied in every respect. We have no desire to have Ayatollahs or Mullahs amongst us. On the contrary, there is a need for tolerance and sound liberalism. But surely there is also a need to have the courage of our convictions when it comes to integrating our religion with secular life.

1 In his **Sociology of Religion**.
2 Paris, Editions Grasset.
3 Cf. article 'Religion without God', in **The Observer** (1963).
4 See P. Berger, **A Rumour of Angels** (New York, 1969).
5 Cf. C. Hartshorne and W. Reese, **Philosophers Speak of God** (Chicago, 1969). See also P. Verhalen, **Faith in a Secularized World: An Investigation into the Survival of Transcendence** (New York, 1976).
6 Cf. also F.C. Happold, **Religious Faith and Twentieth Century Man** (with foreword by John Macquarie) (New York, 1981).
7 First published in 1971.
8 J. Hitchcock, **The Recovery of the Sacred** (New York, 1974).
9 Chateaubriand, **Génie du Christianisme** (Paris, 1802).
10 Joyce O'Connor and Mary Daly, **The West Limerick Study: A Baseline Study of Transition and Change** (Limerick, 1983).
11 C. Arnsberg and S. Kimball, **Family and Community in Ireland** (Cambridge, Mass., 1938).
12 Cf. L. Muir, in Julius Gould (ed.), **The Penguin Survey of the Social Sciences** (London, 1965).
13 M. Mead (New York, 1959).
14 M. Mead (London, 1970).
15 M. Mead (New York, 1955).
16 J. Newman (Dublin, 1966).
17 Cf. Joseph and Frances Gies, **Life in a Medieval City** (New York, 1969).
18 Cf. Gies, **op. cit.**; also Arthur Bryant, **The Medieval Foundation of England** (London, 1966).
19 In R. Bocock and others, **An Introduction to Sociology** (London, 1980).
20 Richard Sennett, **The Uses of Disorder: Personal Identity and City Life** (New York, 1970), p.52.
21 John Laffin, **The Dagger of Islam** (London, 1979), p.29; cf. also G.H. Jansen, **Militant Islam** (London, 1979); L. Babulesco and P. Cardinal, **L'Islam en Questions** (Paris, 1986); Peter Scholl-Latour, **Les Guerriers d'Allah** (Paris, 1986).

Conclusion

Despite the many difficulties in the way of religion that arise from the texture of modern society, there should be no reason for Christians to lose heart. Their faith in the Church as mystery embraces belief in its indefectibility, something that is as true as it is oftentimes hard to credit, just as are the marks of the Church as one, holy, catholic and apostolic.

But it is equally worthy of note that, from the point of view of historical experience, the Church has never been perfect in the concrete. Rather has the case been that it has reflected the features (bad as well as good) of the various epochs of its existence.

THE PAST HAD ITS DEFECTS

A lot is often made today of the lack of understanding of the faith on the part of large masses of people, due as much to new-fangled catechetical methods and poor preaching as it is to the diffusion of secular urban culture. What is scarcely ever recognized is that during the Dark Ages and even the High Middle Ages, the great bulk of the then mainly rural folk had anything but a good understanding of their faith. It could scarcely be otherwise in a period in which ignorance and illiteracy were the order of the day[1]. Indeed so far was it from being the case that proper catechetical instruction was widely available that, on the contrary, the Church had to resort to the inculcation of Christian truth by way of stone sculptures, woodcarvings and stained-glass windows in the churches.

137

There was also moral non-conformity and superstition in abundance, of which readers of Emmanuel Le Roy Ladurie's **Montaillou** will be well aware[2].

The practice of worship also left much to be desired, even in the much vaunted period of Medieval Christendom. It is true that it was this period that saw the erection of the great cathedrals of Europe, yet more and more evidence is beginning to emerge that the 'age of faith', as it is called, was not without many blemishes. The cathedrals were filled only on the great festivals while the multiplicity of smaller churches around them generally betokened the fulfilment of pious works by wealthy benefactors rather than a coping with the spiritual needs of the populace. Renaissance and Reformation periods were also no paragons of Christian living[3]. Nor was the Ancien Régime or the nineteenth century[4].

All this only goes to emphasise the fact that we have to take things in perspective, to recall history and not to expect too much from even convinced believers. There is great danger in indentifying the Church in which one grew up with the Church for all times as far as the pattern of faith and practice is concerned. This is even more so as regards popular piety and devotions, and the rubrics of the liturgy. Indeed it is largely a failure to appreciate the historical dimension of change in the liturgy that has led people astray concerning the importance of the Tridentine Mass. In point of fact, the externals of the Mass have always been subject to change. Perhaps the most striking has been related to the Eucharist. Time was when its reception was regarded as an accepted part of the Mass, reception in the hand at that. In the Late Middle Ages, this emphasis was to yield place more to the veneration of the sacred species at Mass, so much so that elevations of the host during it (at one time as numerous as five) had to be curbed, while communion fell away sharply. This was the period (the fifteenth century) that saw the introduction of Benediction of the Blessed Sacrament as we know it; one cannot find a monstrance that dates from earlier than the fourteenth century. Fourteen centuries of Christians worked out their salvation without the help of such exposition of the Eucharist[5].

THE FUTURE HAS ITS HOPE

And so it is with many other aspects of the Christian religion. At times reception of the sacrament of Penance has been more common than at others. Generally speaking its ups and downs have gone hand in hand with a greater or lesser stress by preachers on sin, death, hell and heaven. The medieval tympanums over many church doors, replete with horned devils and tortured souls, were well calculated to spur people to repentance in a way that modern abstract church art simply does not touch. So too the content of sermons. But if people were not such great sinners in the old days as to warrant terrifying reminders of damnation, neither are we in our day such great saints as to need no reminder of it and to neglect confession.

A balance has to be struck in the religious as in other spheres of life. The fact that the rosary is less said today than formerly does not warrant adopting an attitude of despair for religion. The rosary was not always known in the Church. Neither was the cult of many saints that were later to become much revered. Heresies and sects have always abounded[6]. On the other hand, today we are witnessing an upsurge in traditional pilgrimages and novenas, of a kind that flatly contradicts secularism, and most interestingly among youth. Hence it is that there is no reason for panic. Rather, while being conscious of the secularist threat, we should be optimistic by reason of our faith and the lessons of history and give leadership.

This is not the place in which to write the history of the many ways and times that Christianity overcame its difficulties both external and internal. The extensive bibliography on this theme which I have given here is intended for those who wish to pursue the matter further for themselves.

To end with a few striking examples. It is remarkable how the most recent historians note that, despite the pull of the flesh and the temptations of the sexual, the faithful and the institutional Church have managed, with nuance, to preserve an attachment to the Christian tradition[7]. So also it should not be missed that recruitment to the clergy, although stymied and reduced at times, has, between the Council of Trent and our time, also shown a capacity for come-back[8]. Even the dress of the clergy has shown a potentiality for sane evolution[9]. And then, there is the Mass, the changes in which so disturb some of the faithful at present. They should get themselves to know and ponder the numerous changes which the liturgy of the Mass experienced over the course of the ages while remaining true to its central meaning[10]. If these things and many like them are remembered, there will be no talk about religion being 'out-dated' in the modern world. The opposite in fact will begin to dawn on people, a consciousness that such thinking is really uninformed and behind the times[11]. A consciousness of this is the first step in a return to the sacred.

1 Cf. E. Germain, 2000 ans d'education de la foi (Paris, 1983).
2 E. Le Roy Ladurie, Montaillou: Cathars and Catholics in a French Village 1294-1324 (Paris, 1978; English translation: London 1980). Cf. also Marie-Jeanne Coloni, Hommes et Chrétiens dans la Societé Medievale (Paris, 1981); Rosalind and Christopher Brooke, Popular Religion in the Middle Ages, (London, 1984); Georges Duby, Le Chevalier, la Femme et le Pretre, (Paris, 1981, English translation. New York, 1983); Jacques Rossiand, 'Prostitution, sexualité, societé dans les villes francaises du XVe siécle', and Jean-Louis Flandrin, 'La vie sexuelle des gens mariés dans l'ancienne societé: de la doctrine de l'Église a la realité des comportements' — both in P. Ariès and A. Béjin, Sexualités Occidentales (Paris, 1982); Pierre-Andre Sigal, L'Homme et le Miracle dans la France medievale (Paris, 1985).
3 Cf. Marie-Jeanne Coloni, Hommes et Chretiens de la Renaissance (Paris, 1982); Lucien Febure, Le Problème de l'Incroyance an 16e Siecle (Paris, 1942 and 1968); Natalie Zemon Davis, The Return of Martin Guerre (Harvard, 1983); Robert Mandrou, De la Culture Populaire aux 17 et 18 siecles (Paris, different editions published in 1964, 1974 and 1985).
4 Cf. Gabriel Le Bras, Études de Sociologie Religieuse (Paris, 1955) and F. Boulard, Problèmes Missionnaires de la France Rurale (Paris, 1945); also Philippe Boutry, Prêtres et paroisses au pays du Curé d'Ars Paris, 1986. This book, covering the period 1815 to 1880 in what might have been regarded as a thoroughly reChristianized area is a veritable mine of information.
5 Cf. Gary Macy, The Theologies of the Eucharist in the Early Scholastic Period (Oxford, 1984).

6   Cf. Jacques Le Goff, **Heresies et Societés dans l'Europe pre-industrielle, 11-18 sieclés** (Paris, 1962).

7   Cf. M. Bernos and others, **Le fruit defendu: les Chrétiens et la sexualite de l'antiquité a nos jours** (Paris, 1985).

8   Cf. P. Pierrand, **Le Pretre Francais, du Concile de Trente a nos jours** (Paris, 1986).

9   Cf. L. Trichet, **Le costume du clergé: ses origines et ses evolution en France d'après les reglements de l'Église** (Paris, 1986).

10 Apart from J. Jungmann's great work **The Mass of the Roman Rite** (Vienna, 1949 and New York, 1951), see the very illuminating recent studies — A Rouet, **La Messe dans l'Histoire** (Paris, 1979); P. Loret, **La Messe, du Christ a Jean Paul II** (Mulhouse), 1981; G. Oury **La Messe Romaine et Le Peuple de Dieu dans l'Histore** (Solesmes, 1981); P. Jounel, **La Messe hier et aujourdhui** (Paris, 1986).

11 Cf. Peter Brown, **The Cult of the Saints** (Chicago, 1981). On the history of Christian spirituality as a whole, see Josef Jungmann, **Histoire de la prière Chrétienne** (translated from the German, Paris, 1972); also Urban T. Holmes, **A History of Christian Spirituality** (New York, 1980); Jordan Aumann, **Christian Spirituality in the Catholic Tradition** (London, 1985).

This book is an essay in socio-religious analysis. Its special interest is the impact of modern society on religion, and in particular on Christianity. It provides a valuable review of the literature on this subject and shows how the Christian tradition is faring and the signs of a 'return to the sacred' — a reversal of the desacralization which many societies have experienced. The book's central ideas reflect the best present-day thinking on sociology on both sides of the Atlantic.

Chapters include:

ECLIPSE OF THE SACRED

SOCIOLOGICAL ASPECTS OF THE CHURCH

THE SECULARIZATION OF LIFE

THE PRIVATIZATION OF LIFE

THE EMERGENCE OF CIVIL RELIGION

REINTEGRATING RELIGION AND LIFE

Jeremiah Newman

was professor of Catholic sociology and later president of Maynooth College. This is his twentieth book on sociology and other themes. He is bishop of Limerick in Ireland.

The cover design by Jarlath Hayes
incorporates a graphic by Terence Gayer.